ORFF-SCHULWERK

Wilhelm Keller

INTRODUCTION
TO
MUSIC FOR CHILDREN

Methodology
Playing the Instruments
Suggestions for Teachers

SMC 271

SCHOTT

ISBN 0-930448-10-3

Translator's Note

This book can be used in combination with both the Hall and Murray English language adaptations of the *Schulwerk*. References to specific exercises and musical pieces correspond wherever possible to those in the original German text and are noted by author, volume, and page. Thus, H:I, 6. refers to the adaptation by Hall, volume I, page 6, and M:IV, 29. indicates the Murray edition, volume IV, page 29.

I would like to thank Professor Keller for making his book available for translation and acknowledge the many people in Salzburg who helped me complete this project.

Susan Kennedy

Foreword to the English translation of *Introduction to Music for Children*

I am very pleased that both my *Introduction to Music for Children* and its supplement "Suggestions for Teachers," orginally compiled for the students at the Orff-Institute, now appear in the English language. I have enjoyed several opportunities to become acquainted with colleagues from English-speaking countries and received from them many helpful suggestions for my own work. I hope my small contribution dealing with the correct way to use the materials and methods of the *Orff-Schulwerk* leads to the fruitful further development of "elementary music education" in English-speaking countries.

With my best greetings and good wishes,

Wilhelm Keller

Salzburg, September 1970.

The present revised edition of *Introduction to Music for Children,* originally published in 1954, is intended to extend and amplify the original edition on the basis of ongoing developments and improvements on the Instrumentarium and the continuing experience of the author and many of his colleagues in the teaching praxis of the *Orff-Schulwerk* since the last writing. Both the unusually fast and, even by optimists, unexpected spread of the *Orff-Schulwerk* beyond the area of German-speaking countries (at this time there are nine foreign-language editions) and the increasing interest shown by doctors, social workers, special educators, and psychologists in this new approach to a musical system of basic education, an approach which potentially includes areas of play therapy as yet unexplored and other areas of therapy already formulated and used successfully (experiments with the deaf and blind, for example) oblige one continually to re-examine the methodological and didactic assumptions of educational practice. The establishment in 1961 of the Orff-Institute at the Mozarteum in Salzburg, to be the headquarters and seminar location for the *Orff-Schulwerk,* and a research center for musical, social, and special education, allows us to observe the current stage of development of the *Orff-Schulwerk* more accurately than was earlier possible.

An introductory book can and must limit itself at this stage in the evolution of its subject matter to practices already tried and confirmed. Details and special problems, possible connections with neighboring musical fields, and other questions can only be touched upon here: they will receive more fundamental treatment in individual supplementary books and publications from the Orff-Institute. Written instructions can never replace the personal teaching and lesson supervision of a good teacher with knowledge and ability in the praxis of the *Orff-Schulwerk:* however, they can and should help both teachers and students prepare and later evaluate their experiences with the *Orff-Schulwerk.*

W. K.

Salzburg, February 1963.

3

This book tries to answer questions asked of the author and his colleagues by educators of all kinds, at conventions, courses, lectures, discussions and other gatherings, about the praxis of the *Orff-Schulwerk*. It further attempts to lessen the danger of misunderstanding and misapprehending the degree of difficulty involved in this new approach to music-making and musical practice by counteracting both overestimation and underestimation of the claims and technical questions presented here.

It addresses itself primarily to grammar school teachers, music teachers in the public schools, professors of music at teacher-training institutions, and, beyond these, also to teachers in middle and high schools, educational centers, and all educators* who support good musical education and feel themselves responsible for it. The concept "Music for Children" should be understood very broadly to include music-making with adolescents at school and at home: the material presented in volumes IV and V will have particular appeal not limited to children. No special musical training is required of the readers of this book other than the knowledge of elementary music education that was part of their general educational training. On the other hand, it is unavoidable that musical and educational platitudes will be discussed in our presentation that some educators perhaps do not want to hear again; we have inserted them nevertheless, mindful of the words of the poet Peter Altenburg, who once said that it is, of course, no art to utter such platitudes; however, it is an unforgiveable sin of omission not to repeat them continually. So, may the experienced accept our presentation as a confirmation and extension of their own knowledge and ability, and the inexperienced take it as their first helper when starting to work with this new tool. This "Introduction" is not a summary of the *Orff-Schulwerk*; it can only supplement it and be used solely in connection with the materials recorded and commented upon there.

W. K.

May 1954

* *see the Foreword to the revised edition for reference to interest groups from the areas of medicine, social — and special education.*

GENERAL COMMENTS

1.

The *Orff-Schulwerk* is a musical contribution to the establishment of a modern system of general education. As such it assumes in students neither special musical ability, nor previous training. On the other hand, it does not restrict genuine talent. Instead, in the variety of its activities, it allows children to try out and confirm their own abilities without sacrificing a common source of musical sound and means appropriate to childhood. Correctly used, the *Orff-Schulwerk* offers worthwhile activities for children with greater and lesser gifts, so no individual is pushed ahead too fast or held back unnecessarily. The real goal of the Schulwerk is attained in one's enjoyment of the fruitful combination of personal and interpersonal resources. Creating, reproducing and listening to music are not separate and exclusive areas of work, but are presented as one entity in the elementary musical experience of all participants. The *Orff-Schulwerk* is not a method; rather, it is an indicator, a signpost. Everything we shall discuss about methods should be viewed according to the principles set out above and understood to represent only a few ways among the many which exist. All our suggestions may be altered at any time to adapt to the circumstances at hand.

2.

The *Orff-Schulwerk* is primarily intended for group work. There are exercises for individuals and "soloistic" passages within the pieces, but there are never soloists who force all the other music makers into the role of accompanying one single predominant voice. The smallest possible group consists of two players who take an equal share in performing or improvising a piece. It is impossible to determine a maximum size for group musical activity. Because this depends on the number of instruments available, the spatial situation, and other circumstances, it can only be stated relatively. It is possible to work equally well with both small and large groups if the musical result of the combined instruments is well supervised and the resulting dynamic level appropriately adjusted. The over-populated school class of today, (about which teachers so often and justly complain), is *no* obstacle for using the *Orff-Schulwerk* if it is handled correctly according to the size of the group. *One* prerequisite is indeed indispensable: the availability of a room which allows all the participants enough freedom to clap, stamp, snap their fingers, and play instruments, and, not least important, which permits the whole group to move and dance. Whenever new schools are built, a special music and gymnastics room should be included in addition to the gymnasium to meet these requirements. If such a room is not already available, the gymnasium or a large all-purpose room can be used; at the very least, the classroom should be transformed into a temporary music room by clearing the largest possible floor space.

3.

Elementary music-making is possible at every age; differences according to age group will be noticed only in the choice of song texts, voice parts, and musical and technical demands. The series *Music for Children,* which we discuss here, is primarily intended for children from six to fourteen years of age. It need hardly be mentioned that it is possible to make music in *Orff-Schulwerk* style with pre-school age children and those beyond age fifteen if the form is appropriately simplified or made more complex. Within the schools, grouping is usually according to age level, since most classes contain children of equal age. Outside of school and at home children will also be able to make music together with the *Orff-Schulwerk.* Moreover, there are completely new possibilities for "Hausmusik" within the family where the parents can also participate.

THE INSTRUMENTARIUM

From the start we use the musical instrument for its original purpose: to provide the rhythmic component of music, combined with the singing voice (the original source of melody). Every person brings natural instruments with him into the world: *hands* and *feet* with which he is able to clap, stamp, and pat on his knees. The limited range of sounds produced by clapping, stamping and knee-patting ("patschen"), finger-snapping, etc., which can have some variety or gradation, is refined, broadened, and liberated when the instrument group of *small percussion instruments* is called into use. In this group we find the rattle, claves, large and small cymbals, triangle, castanets, different kinds of wood blocks and skin drums, bells, and related instruments.

In addition to these instruments which lack adjustable pitch and function as pure sound and rhythm producers, there are percussion instruments with adjustable pitch: small drums, kettledrums, timpani, bar instruments and tuned glasses. The bar instruments (glockenspiel, metallophone, and xylophone, plus the tuned glasses) constitute a bridge between melodic and rhythmic instruments, and, thus, form the core of the whole body of instruments.

Stringed instruments, bowed and plucked, form a third group: gambas and "fidels" (six-stringed instruments in different voices), psalteries, lutes, and guitars. The tenor and bass fidels, gamba, 'cello, and contra-bass function as bass instruments along with the drums, bass xylophone and a bordun instrument currently in the experimental stage. In the volumes of *Music for Children,* these voices, intended for varied instrumentation, are uniformly notated as "bass."

Wind instruments form the last group to be mentioned: recorders and bamboo flutes, sordune, krummhorns, rauschpfeifes, and others.

PLAYING TECHNIQUES FOR PERCUSSION INSTRUMENTS

Conducting exercises

We include conducting under playing percussion instruments, because in *Music for Children* the conductor has no other function than that of a central percussionist, who, as "concertmaster," leads the group rhythmically. Conducting exercises are introduced together with exercises for clapping, stamping, knee-patting, and finger-snapping discussed below. Conducting should always give rhythmic direction and accompany speaking and singing exercises. All students should take part in conducting lessons so that they can all ultimately assume the duties of director. We follow conducting methods used internationally for basic rhythm patterns, using both hands mirroring each other, without a baton, as is the practice in choral conducting:

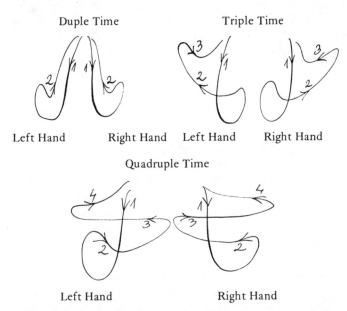

Duple Time   Triple Time

Left Hand   Right Hand   Left Hand   Right Hand

Quadruple Time

Left Hand   Right Hand

To begin, the conductor raises both arms so that his upper-arms are almost at shoulder level, but the shoulders are not raised. His lower arms turn inward so the hands almost touch each other. The fingers are closed (as though they were holding teacups), and the backs of the hands are upward. This basic hand-position is maintained throughout the measure. The hands should not turn around.

In the performance of the measure the wrist is relaxed and the fingers are closed, but not cramped. The conductor should imagine a lower plane for the beat a little above the center of his body and strike it with a bouncing downward motion. He conducts away from his body, never in a nervous defensive position, and bends a little forward. At every change of direction in the beat pattern (see the graphic illustrations above), the wrist makes a small tossing motion. When the piece begins with a downbeat, the conductor anticipates with an upbeat gesture:

Pear - tree

If it begins with a full up-beat, he gives the preceding full beat value before the entrance:

Oh   why

If it begins with an upbeat of less than one full beat value, he subdivides the beat with an energetic movement to indicate the entrance:

Ma - ri - a

The cut-off at the end of a piece or section is most successfully indicated by a bouncing circular movement outward on the last beat, so that the hands return to their initial position. We strongly advise the teacher to inform and train himself further in the conducting techniques only briefly mentioned here, either by reading a textbook about choral conducting or, better still, by participating in a conducting course. He should not only be able to lead a musical group correctly by himself, but also to pass on the techniques to his students, and guide and correct them.

Clapping

Even clapping needs to be practiced and studied. The person clapping must move his hands and arms with an elastic stroke in combination with correct breathing. Clapping exercises are best begun in a standing position, so the arms can move with a relaxed pendulum swing. The clap itself can either be double-sided on a diagonal line (right hand moving from the right side to the left hand below; left hand from the left side below to hit the right hand above), or one-sided (one hand clapping against the other palm which is calmly held opposite). The person clapping should always be relaxed, as should the conductor. Clapping itself requires a minimum of strength.

We make a distinction between *hollow* and *flat* clapping according to the position of the palms of the hands and the type of clap that is performed. For hollow clapping the hands are cupped like shells. When they clap together a vacuum is created and a hollow sound produced. In flat clapping the fingers are straight. Here the one-sided clap of right hand onto left palm is recommended. The palm itself has different clapping surfaces: a clap in the middle or against the fingers of the left hand sounds different from a clap in the wrist area or against the edge of the palm. All varieties of clapping should be discovered and used.

It is important to observe all dynamic gradations, especially transitions from *piano* to *forte* and the reverse ("crescendo" and "decrescendo"). *Piano* clapping is more important than *forte*, because it makes it necessary for the clapper to listen to the other people in the group. This keenness of hearing helps refine the color differences in the sounds produced. *Piano clapping must not lead to rhythmic imprecision.* At the beginning this often indicates an incorrect attitude about the concept itself: *piano does not means lack of concentration!* Intensity, especially rhythmic intensity, must be part of even the softest degree of sound. (These ground rules are true for all work with every instrument no matter what its nature.)

Knee-patting ("Patschen")

By "patschen" we mean patting with flat hands on the thighs. Patschen creates a new tone color, and it can be used alone or in combination with clapping and stamping. Here, as everywhere in music-making, the body is relaxed, but "ready-to-spring," a bearing common to all exercises calling for athletic or dancelike motion. Patschen may be done while seated or standing.

8

Finger-snapping

In every group there will be a number of dextrous finger-snappers; the rest will learn it immediately or never, for not every hand is suited for this activity. It is important that finger-snapping not come from a stiff hand and arm position, but always be relaxed and swinging.

Stamping

The children can either sit or stand for stamping. If they stand, they first raise their feet by lifting the underleg lightly backward, and then stamp on the foot-swing forward. After the stamp the foot should stay on the floor. (A child will tend to raise his foot again and stand helplessly.) In addition to this "full-stamp," the children should practice tapping their toes while their heels stay on the floor, and vice versa, tapping their heels with toes fixed on the floor.

Rattle

The rattle is a simple percussion instrument that any child can make by filling a hollow body, (tin or wood box, paper tube, coconut shell, gourd), with some moveable stuffing, (sand, small stones, metal scraps, rice, dried beans). The instrument gets its name from the rattling sound it makes when it is shaken or struck. The correct amount of filling for a rattle can be judged by trying out various amounts and listening to the sound. The instrument should be comfortable to hold in one hand in a manner that does not mute its sound.

Woodblock

The name of this instrument describes both its material and structure. It is played with beaters with hard felt, wood or rubber heads. The box-shaped instrument should sit with the slit upward on a base or mat that does not dampen its sound. The best place to strike the instrument is directly above the slit. The hard clear sound of the wood block, which is built in different sizes, should be used sparingly, so its unique value is not lessened through overuse. A special variety of the wood block is known as "temple blocks."

Claves

The name "claves" denotes a pair of sticks made of resonant wood, bamboo, or some other material. To play the claves the person strikes the sticks against each other while holding them lightly between his thumbs and index fingers. For a more intense sound the thumb and index finger of the left hand may hold one stick. The hand is cupped into a hollow shape, so that the stick extends along the finger tips to mid-wrist. It is struck by the other stick held in the right hand.

Like the other small percussion instruments, claves are especially suited for use when the player is moving about.

Castanets

This ancient "clapper" is known today primarily as a Spanish folk instrument. Castanets are two hardwood shells bound together by string. They are played in pairs to accompany dancing. Correct technique for playing this type of castanets is an art in itself. The shells are held by the string between the middle finger and thumb and brought together by appropriate finger movement. We prefer to use the so-called "shake" or "stick" castanets with the shells mounted on a handle. To play precise rhythms and prevent unwanted sounds it is best to use only one instrument. The right hand holds the instrument and beats it against the left palm.

Its penetrating sound should not be over-used.

Large and small cymbals

Cymbals, large and small, are instruments, or, more precisely, pairs of instruments made out of circular metal platters, shells, and discs with rims that vibrate while the depressed center area remains still. Each cymbal has a hand-strap that does not interfere with its sound. The name "cymbal" is old, and today it has several meanings. In general it describes smaller instruments, often worked into shell-shapes or made of hard alloys. The smallest form of cymbal is the "finger-cymbal." The Italian "piatti" (German: "Becken") are flatter, larger, disc-shaped, and made of softer material. Cymbals smaller than those found in the orchestra are manufactured for making music with children. Between *Chinese* and *Turkish* cymbals there is a further structural difference. The Chinese cymbals have upward-bent edges, are thinner, and sound less full than the flatter Turkish cymbals, made of a better alloy. Both large and small cymbals can be made to sound when the two hands bring them crashing together. In the musical score these double cymbals are indicated: -| |-, the hanging cymbal: ⊥ . When the cymbal clash is for rhythmic accent or climax, the two cymbals are brought together by a circular upward hand movement. If an accompaniment or subdivided figure with softer sound is intended, the cymbals glance together vertically, up and down. The loops are held securely so the cymbals cannot dangle out of control and create extra noise. No other percussion instrument is more tempting to *misuse* than the cymbal! Our own suggestion is to start playing softly and gradually increase the dynamic level. For another playing technique, one cymbal is fastened on a suitable stand so it hangs freely, or held high from its loop handle in the left hand, and struck with a beater held in the right hand, either on the rim, from above, or from the side. The cymbal may continue to ring, or be silenced by the player's grasping its rim, indicated in the score: /. A "rustling" effect is obtained by playing a roll on a large cymbal with soft beaters. The rim of one cymbal itself becomes a "beater" when it is carefully made to strike against the rim of the other cymbal.

Finger cymbals are placed on the thumb and middle finger of one hand, and struck bouncingly together. One player can play two pairs. They are especially suited for playing while a person is moving or dancing. Another way to play them involves holding one cymbal in each hand so that they dangle. The cymbals are brought to sound by hitting the edge of one against the other from above.

Triangle

The triangle, a three-cornered bent metal bar, hangs from one of its angles by a thread or piece of gut string. The left hand holds it high, and the right hand strikes it lightly with a metal beater. Thin or weak beaters give a comparably softer sound. Only careful experimentation and listening can differentiate between usuable and inappropriate sounds. The instrument comes in different sizes. Its sound is characteristically very adaptable to the tonal color of other instruments, and, therefore, it combines well with them. Used in combination with the glockenspiel, the cymbals, or other instruments, the triangle seems to take on their properties of sound. The triangle is normally played on its horizontal section, but it is possible to use all three sides. A tremolo is played by striking the triangle quickly back and forth on the inside.

Frame drum (Tambour)

Frame drums are single-headed drums with a natural skin stretched over a wooden frame. They are available in various sizes, with or without tension screws. We do not recommend drums without tension screws because they are often inferior in quality and quickly become unusable. Jingles may be built into the frame, and there are some models which allow the jingles to be added or taken out as desired. A frame drum with jingles ("Schellentrommel") is known in English-speaking countries as a tambourine.

The frame drum is played either with the hand or with beaters. Only in the first instance is the name "hand drum" proper. This term does not indicate a certain instrument, but a certain playing technique. Familiarity with the most important beating techniques is indispensable. Especially important: the drum is held by the left hand, either in a hanging position at waist-level, or held high and firmly so that the drum's lower edge is approximately at eye-level. The hanging position is used only when the player is standing, because it requires freedom of movement. The other position can be used when the player is seated. This high position requires more strength than the other, although the frame drum is comparatively light in weight. It encourages intense and concentrated playing and should be used particularly whenever the drum is the leading element in the ensemble. (In primitive cultures this position is always used to accompany dancing.) The hanging position is more comfortable and only requires firmer pressure of the hand holding the drum to prevent the instrument from swaying freely in the hand or dangling altogether, at the expense of tone and rhythmic accuracy.

In playing the hand drum the primary "beaters" are the thumb and the last three fingers. If we want the effect of a hard beater we use the extended thumb and middle finger, which then become a "pair of beaters" and play alternately. Finally, if a more muted sound is called for, the ball-of-the-hand or the inside of the wrist (the under-edge of the palm) may serve as beater "heads," with the fingers bent backward. Because every hand is unique, each player must discover his own best solution for each type of beat. It is important to know which area of the drumhead produces a certain kind of sound. The edge of the drumhead is the most resonant. The frame is an integral part of the drum and resonates itself, so it may also be struck. (In good instruments the tone thus produced will not be inferior to that produced when the membrane is struck.) Here, too, only experimentation with an instrument can determine its best playing areas. The least resonance comes from the center of the drum head. Between the center and the edge of the membrane many transitional colors can be produced. These should all be used. By consciously using different areas of the drum head the player can create sounds from the finest differentiations up to the great contrast between center and edge sounds.

There are several different techniques for striking the drum: the *finger stroke*, *ball-of-hand stroke, thumb stroke, small alternating stroke,* and *large alternating stroke.* The *finger stroke,* mentioned above, is done either with extended fingers or with fingers fanned out from the little finger. The entire arm swings to produce the stroke, and the wrist is decisive because the real impulse for the stroke originates in its movements:

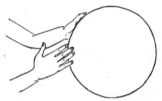

It is possible to use the ball-of-hand as an independent type of stroke, but it is more commonly used in combination with the finger-stroke. In the *small alternating stroke* the hand is extended, the thumb stretched as far as possible away from the middle finger. When the wrist moves back and forth, the thumb and extended fingers strike the edge of the drum head in alternation. This is best carried out when the drum is held high, and constitutes the most important technique for playing fast sub-divided rhythms. A roll is produced when the wrist moves quickly back and forth. This is an excellent exercise to train relaxed playing. The player starts with small alternating strokes of equal size and builds gradually to the desired tempo.

The goal here is to achieve the most consistent dynamic level when using this alternating stroke, not allowing any dynamic unevenness to be heard. Another type of small alternating stroke comes from the alternation of the finger and ball-of-hand strokes. This requires two different playing areas of the drum to be used, because the wrist or ball-of-hand will strike a little farther into the center of the drum head than the fingers. Because this technique does not originate from a simple swinging or shaking movement, it requires considerable ability and strength. Therefore, we prefer to use it in two-handed playing, which we discuss later.

The *large alternating stroke* is used only when the drum is in a hanging position. It involves striking opposite sides of the drum head, not only the edge areas. The alternation is between finger and thumb or ball-of-hand strokes. If a hollow unresonating sound is desired, the middle of the membrane should be used. The finger stroke itself provides the impulse for the thumb stroke. The large alternating stroke is appropriate for sequences in moderate tempo where variations of dynamics and color are important. The ball-of-hand stroke produces a good accent, although the player should also practice it in an unaccented pattern. This stroke can just as well provide the push-off impulse for the succeeding finger stroke.

Finally, talented players can perform fast passages by playing with all ten fingers on the drum head (as if on a keyboard instrument), if even and not too loud figures are required. We further recommend *two-handed* drum playing where the drum is held between the player's knees and tilted a little forward. Small double drums are most appropriate for this kind of technique. Frame drums suffer dampened sound whenever the frame is grasped, because its vibration is affected. For two-handed playing, use the ball-of-hand stroke in alternation with the finger stroke discussed above.

When the player is standing it is possible for him to hold the drum between his left underarm and hip, so that his left hand is free to play the drum with beaters. His right hand can play the drum with or without beaters.

To play the frame drum with beaters, no additional information is necessary concerning what areas of the drum head to use. The tonal color produced, the energy required, and the degree of volume resulting all depend on the quality of the particular drum and beaters. If it is impossible to have a variety of beaters on hand, the best choice for a frame drum is a beater with a soft felt head. The sound of a beater with a hard felt or wooden head is easier to approximate with fingers and thumb than is this softer sound.

Tambourine (Schellentrommel)
This drum can be played exactly like the frame drum without jingles, that is, like a hand drum. In this way, the jingles supply accompanying color. If they should sound more

strongly or characteristically, the drum is played with an exaggerated shake. Both skin and jingles come into play when the drum is struck with the hand or across the knee. A kind of drum roll is produced by rubbing the edge of the drum head with a dampened thumb, which then acts with springing movement. To play the drum with both hands, place it across the knees and use both hands on the edge of the drum head.

Sleigh bells
Fastened on the wrist, foot, or elsewhere, or held freely in the hand, the sleigh bells add accompanying color to clapping, stamping, and knee-patting. They can also be used independently.

Jingles rattle
On the jingles rattle the jingles are mounted in a wooden frame with a handle. They are usually arranged in pairs as they are on the jingles drum (tambourine) to hit against each other when the instrument is moved. The rattle is either shaken or struck with the free hand.

Side drum (Snare drum)
The side drum is a double-headed drum, used with or without snares. Smaller more simple versions of this instrument are built for children and young people. If no stand is available for the drum it must be placed at the knee-level of the seated player. The drum head slants slightly sideward, tilted toward the player. The side drum has its own pair of wooden drumsticks (not to be confused with wooden-headed beaters) each made from a single piece of wood. Their thicker handles taper at the opposite end to an egg-shaped tip. These sticks are usually supplied with the drum. Correct handling of this drum is one of the most critical problems in percussion technique. We have room to mention only the most important things here, including a few suggestions for simplified playing techniques. Merely holding the sticks, especially the left one, is difficult for children. The left stick lies between the thumb and upper edge of the center of the hand. Index and middle fingers are bent loosely, not touching the stick. It rests on the fourth finger and extends a few centimeters beyond the hand. The right hand holds its drumstick from above with the thumb, index finger, and possibly the middle finger. The remaining fingers curve without touching the drumstick, which, this time, does not extend beyond the hand:

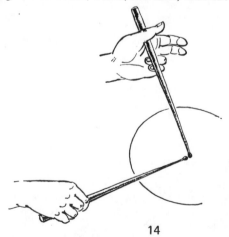

Students with greater ability can experiment with and practice this original drumstick position. Less able ones may hold the left stick in the same way as the right. (Professional players also adopt this second technique when they use several drums or kinds of beaters.) The side drum's characteristic sound is the result of trilling or bouncing strokes made possible, almost spontaneous, by the elasticity of the drumhead and the player's loose grip on the drumsticks. This roll is not achieved in the same way on the side drum as it is on other percussion instruments, i.e. by quickly alternating single beats. Rather, it comes from alternating double (repeated) beats. These must be practiced slowly at first, then accelerated by subdividing figures until the roll is accomplished.

Keeping this roll under control is the greatest problem. The player should not pull away when striking the drumhead. He must move the sticks from his wrists down onto the surface of the drum and raise them similarly without letting them skitter back and forth. The side drum is played primarily in the center of its drumhead, in contrast to the practice for the more loosely stretched membrane of the frame drum. The only time the drumsticks glide from the edge to the middle and back again is to produce crescendo and decrescendo during the roll.

Characteristic of the side drum is the "rattle" effect produced by the snares located on the underside of the drum. They give special color to the drum roll. The side drum can also be used without the snare. The sound then resembles that of other drums with stretched skin drumheads.

Special drums and other percussion instruments

Larger double-headed drums (variations of the "bass drum" of the orchestra) sit on their cylindrical bodies in front of the player, who can play on both heads from both left and right sides. All kinds of beaters may be used with these drums if everything we have mentioned for playing hand drums is taken into account. The drums we know today from jazz and dance music, such as the bongos, conga drums, tomtoms, and other sounding instruments can be including in making music with the *Schulwerk*. The playing techniques we discussed above are also valid for these instruments. Every land and culture has its own percussion instruments. They should be used both in their characteristic forms and appropriateness for certain musical styles, and also experimentally in all possible new combinations.

Bar instruments

In this category we mean percussion instruments made of a resonance chamber and a row of specifically tuned sounding bars of wood or metal, played with beaters. Bar instruments of wood are called *xylophones;* those with metal bars, *glockenspiels,* and *metallophones.* Xylophones have various forms and ranges. For our work the soprano and alto xylophones are the most important. Lower instruments (tenor and bass xylophones) enrich and complete the xylophone family. Among the metal bar instruments the soprano and alto glockenspiels are the most important. The name "glockenspiel" describes the bell-like sound of the hard metal bars, usually made of nickel-plated steel. The metallophones could be called "deep glockenspiels" and the name "metallophone" generalized to include all metal instruments. But the designation metallophone has become accepted to mean bar instruments whose bars are made of light metal alloy. The sound of these bars is dark, soft, and known by long reverberation. Metallophones are also built in several sizes, most frequently in two ranges, soprano and alto, to correspond to the soprano and alto xylophones.

The form of the bar instruments used in the *Orff-Schulwerk*, constituting, as we mentioned earlier, the very core of the Instrumentarium, was first created in 1930 by the Munich instrument builder Karl Maendler, at the inspiration and suggestion of Carl Orff.

The basic tonality of the bar instruments is C major. Substitute bars are available for the tones F-sharp, B-flat, C-sharp, and, if desired, for all the other pitches needed to build a tempered half-tone row. These extra bars make possible modulations into neighboring keys or complete transpositions from one key into another. A "transposing instrument" can be constructed by rearranging the bars equally. (More about that later.)

Diatonic bar instruments can be converted into chromatic instruments by adding an extra chromatic resonance box with those tones which do not belong to the diatonic instrument, corresponding to the black keys on the piano. The following notation gives an overview of the ranges of the bar instruments in notation and also shows the true sound of the instruments:

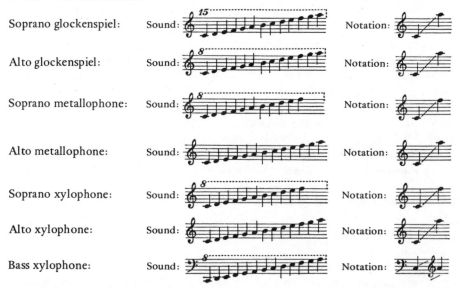

To change a bar instrument into a transposing instrument, as we mentioned above, the lowest tone of the new key must be placed in the lowest position on the instrument. The new scale is then constructed upward from this lowest bar. For example, to change from

C to D we place the lowest D-bar where the lowest (longest) C-bar originally stood and build the D scale upward from there.* In the pentatonic, steps IV and VII are omitted, so their corresponding bars are also left out. Their places on the instrument are left unoccupied to provide a spatial reminder of the interval of the minor third. In the key of C, bars F and B stay out; in D, bars G and C-sharp. In both the keys of C and D, however, the open (unoccupied) spaces on the instrument are in the same place, because in both keys the lowest tone of the scale is in the first (lowest) position on the instrument. For the player, nothing is different. He plays as though still in C, while the actual sound of the instrument has been transposed in D.

This kind of transposition of the entire tonal range can be carried out at any time. It is especially called for when the C notation coincides with the lowest limit of the child's voice, in which case transposition upward is required. All the songs in the *Orff-Schulwerk* can be sung at their absolute notated pitch. Yet transposition upward is always permissible whenever the basic tonality of the instruments (in absolute notation) requires too deep a range for children's voices. Relative notation is the rule.

Playing the bar instruments

The instrument should sit on a proper stand so that the playing surface lies approximately at the player's knee-level. The lower bars of the instrument lie to the player's left, as they would with a keyboard instrument. To play while standing the playing surface must be at the player's waist-level.

The bar instruments are played with a pair of beaters held so that the backs of the player's hands are upward. In another position sometimes used by professional percussion players and especially suited for virtuoso performance, the hands grip the handles of the beaters from underneath with thumbs on top. For this second position, handles with flat grips are best. If possible, the handle should have an indentation for the thumb. (This feature is, or was, required for the "spoon" beaters of the orchestral xylophone.) The handle of these beaters is held between the index and middle fingers with the thumb above.

On the basis of past experience we recommend using the first position for elementary music-making with children: that is, with the backs of the hands upward. (Nothing against the other position is intended. It is always permissible if it produces satisfactory tonal and rhythmic results.) For the simpler grip, the beaters are held firmly with the thumb, index and middle fingers, so that they lie between the first and middle joints of

---

* *Impairment of resonance caused by this displacement is hardly noticeable. If it is disturbing, the D scale may be built upward from the original position of the lowest D bar.*

the two fingers. They are not to be held by the fingertips, grasped with the whole hand, or taken with the fist:

The fourth and fifth fingers curve loosely around the end of the stick. A beginner will tend to put his index finger on top of the stick to feel more secure with them. This mistake causes a stiff grip and unelastic stroke, which can strangle the resonance of the bar. The player must try to avoid this position completely and to correct it immediately if it does occur. When held correctly the beaters incline inward before the stroke, following the natural position of the hands:

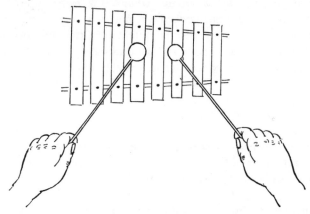

The stroke itself must be short and bouncing. Otherwise, as we have already mentioned, the heads of the beaters bring the vibration of the bar to a standstill and completely deaden the sound. The player should strike the bar in the center, concentrating on moving his arms and wrists in a relaxed "waving" or "flying" ("winglike") way. The stroke is first learned with both hands together, with the arms evenly raised. Then each hand practices independently. Finally, the two hands alternate in an evenly-measured succession of strokes. This left and right alternation will later become the basic technique for playing melodies. We will explain further how the bordun and ostinato figures in the musical pieces and exercises in the *Schulwerk* volumes provide ample opportunities for practicing this alternating stroke.

In addition to the normal stroke using one beater in each hand, the "fork-grip" makes it possible to play a double stroke with two beaters in each hand. To do this the two beaters are taken in one hand with the index finger (or, for wider intervals, both index and middle fingers) bent in between the two sticks. The other fingers hold the ends of the beaters fast in the deepest point of the inside of the palm, so the sticks cannot collide with each other and make disturbing extraneous sounds. It is very important that this position not make the hands cramp, a common hazard because of the firm grip this is necessary. By using the "fork-grip" with both hands (i.e. with four beaters), one player can play a four-voiced chord. (The fork-grip is introduced only after the regular grip no longer causes any difficulties.)

We introduce the "cross-over" stroke early because it trains the two hands to work independently. In the simplest cross-over stroke one hand plays a middle tone repeatedly, and the other alternates with it, playing first a lower then a higher tone in a slow tempo to the left and right of the repeated tone. There is also sufficient material for these and similar exercises among the bordun and ostinato figures in the *Schulwerk* volumes. During the cross-over stroke the beaters may not touch each other. They must be held almost parallel to each other, at right angles to the tone bars. The handles should never touch the bars. (This cannot happen when the beaters are held correctly.)

Finally, there are other techniques that can be used opportunely and economically to create special effects on the bar instruments: the *glissando* and the *tremolo*. The glissando has a definite opening and closing stroke: in between them the beater is drawn lightly over the row of tone bars. The initial and final strokes are always played with beater *not* playing the glissando itself. They precede and follow the glissando immediately, without a split-second of hesitation. For the tremolo, two beaters strike the same tone bar in rapid alternation. It should be practiced slowly at first. To play a *glissando*, the beaters are loosely held and the wrists are kept relaxed and flexible so they can glide the beaters across the bars without interruptions. The player can also make use of the elastic quality of the bars for the *tremolo*, without sacrificing his control of the beaters.

Many kinds of beaters can be used to play the bar instruments, although each kind of instrument does have a characteristic beater which corresponds best to its structural qualities. Xylophone beaters are usually made with hard felt or rubber heads. Wooden-headed or spoon beaters are only used occasionally to make a harder sound for musical or textual emphasis. In contrast, the glockenspiel is usually played with wooden-headed beaters, and occasionally with small metal hammers. Small wooden hammers are now available with a patch of felt glued to one side, so one hammer can produce two different qualities of sound. The felt side dampens the sound and makes the glockenspiel sound more like the metallophone, which is itself played with hard felt (xylophone) beaters.

In general, the metal instruments should be played more softly and carefully than the wooden xylophones, (which is not to suggest that xylophones can be handled carelessly!). The metal instruments produce a more intense sound, and they can easily become overbearing and predominant. For the same reason they should be used economically in a musical piece, so their sound does not become noise.

Musical glasses
This homemade instrument can be an addition to the glockenspiel family. One can collect tumblers or goblets in many sizes which have a good ring, so that each corresponds to a definite pitch when struck. The glasses are then arranged into a tone row like that on the bar instruments. Filling the glass with water will lower the pitch it produces approximately one half-step. It is good to assemble the complete pentatonic (five-tone) row, although fewer tones may also be used. Even a single tone will work if it corresponds to a tone found in the basic triad of the scale in use. (In C, it could be c, g, or e.) The

musical glasses are played with wooden-headed (xylophone) beaters, held by three fingers. The player stands and strikes the glasses very lightly on their rims, using only the strength of the weight of the beaters.

The player can also make the glasses "sing," an effect like the sound of the glockenspiel, if he rubs their rims lightly with moistened fingertips. This is the sound of the "glass harmonica" which long ago entranced Goethe.

Small kettle drums

Small kettle drums (also called small timpani) differ from the large kettle drums of the orchestra not only in size but also in the style of their construction. They are single-headed cylindrical drums with definite, and, within certain limits, adjustable pitch. They are best used in pairs, or in groups of three or four drums of different sizes. They are tuned to the interval of a fourth or fifth, or to two other pitches important in the desired key. One should practice the tuning process: be sure to pay attention to keeping even tension and loosening of the drumhead by adjusting all the tension screws in the same direction. First turn two screws located opposite to each other across the drumhead until the desired pitch is reached. Afterward, tighten all the other screws (again in opposing pairs) accordingly. Unfortunately, no single standard type of small kettle drum is available, and tonal ranges and ways to tune the instruments vary according to their manufacturer. Specific information about the drum's range, limits (especially the upper range limit), and tuning is available from the manufacturer or can be discovered by experimenting with the drum. It may be necessary to tune the smaller drum to the fundamental tone and the larger drum to the dominant, as a lower fourth. On other instruments, it can be possible to assign the fundamental tone to the deeper drum and the fifth to the smaller (upper dominant). The drums can also be tuned to other steps of the scale, for example, to degrees I and II.

These drums are played with all kinds of beaters; usually the beaters have semi-soft heads of felt, or leather with soft stuffing (timpani sticks). The sticks are held like those for the bar instruments; the backs of the hands may also be held to the side. Although it is customary to place the higher drum to the left of the player and the lower drum to his right, we recommend another position that corresponds to the arrangement of the bar instruments: that is, to the left of the player the lower drum, to his right the higher drum. This keeps the layout constant for the whole Instrumentarium and is desirable since all the players should learn to use all of the instruments, and no child should become a specialist on only one.

The playing surface of these drums is so constructed that they are always played at the edge of the drumhead.

If large kettle drums are available they may be used with careful attention to dynamics. This is also true for other large percussion instruments, the bass drum, large cymbals, snare drums, and their relatives. The sound of the timpani and drums can be partially muted by covering a section of the drumhead with a cloth or felt strip.

USING OTHER INSTRUMENTS

Bass instruments

In addition to the simple bordun instrument and the low xylophone which we have already mentioned, the stringed instruments may be used as primary bass instruments. To play a simple bordun, the player tunes the two lowest strings to the fundamental and the fifth of the given key. The other strings can either be tuned to double this bordun fifth or to play supplemental tones of any chord. No knowledge of any fingering technique is required to pluck a simple bordun on open strings. If there are string players among the group, the bordun accompaniment need not be limited to open strings. The player can expand and vary the bordun with fingering and legato bowing to play longer tones (pedal point).

Keyboard instruments

The question concerning whether the piano, small organ, harpsichord, or clavichord should be used arises primarily when no other instruments are available. The wide tonal range commanded by these instruments can tempt one to include them. Expanding the music-making group with these instruments is done almost certainly at the cost of the unity and purity of the group's musical style. For this reason at the beginning of Vol. I, we caution against using the piano, but we do recognize the older keyboard instruments (harpsichord and clavichord) as alternate instruments to those of the Instrumentarium, because of the quality of their sound. Because of its soft sound, the clavichord is not suited for making music with large groups. It can be used occasionally as a sound register in combination with other softly sounding instruments. The harpsichord fits in the best with the sound of the Instrumentarium. It lacks a mechanism for espressivo attack and stays dynamically constant within a chosen register. So the harpsichord can give support at every level of pitch without bringing in sounds that are foreign to the entire style. Despite these advantages and possibilities, we warn against making too much use of such a versatile instrument. The temptation is great to retreat from making music with the whole group to merely accompanying a song with a keyboard instrument and a few extra percussion instruments, to spare oneself the trouble of working out a piece with a homogeneous body of instruments.

What is not a problem with the harpsichord, because of its mechanics and sound quality, does become a source of disturbance with the piano, that is, the very versatility of dynamics and tone color resources within its basic sound. It should be used solely within the children's own tonal realm and then only with very cautious adaptation to the sound of the Orff Instrumentarium to emphasize that side of its characteristic sound that blends well with the tonal quality of metal bar instruments. Even then it should be used only when absolutely necessary. We completely exclude accordions and harmonicas because they contradict the musical ideals of the *Orff-Schulwerk* both in character and playing technique.

Bowed and plucked instruments

In addition to the singing voice and the wind instruments mentioned above, (see the relevant literature for playing techniques), another melodic instrument should be mentioned which has recently come to the fore: the "fidel." These instruments mix outstandingly well with the sounds of the bar instruments and the small percussion. Older children (ten years old and above) can form a fidel-group within the larger music-making body. Their contribution will serve to hold the percussion players to sensitive production of tone. This is also true of psalteries, with different styles of construction, and other plucked instruments. These may be inserted as melodic as well as accompanying instruments. Violins and violas are too demanding in playing technique and too apt to lead one to expressive playing (in the sense of "art music") which can be poorly reconciled with elementary music-making. Therefore they are better used not as leading melodic instruments, but to enrich or complement accompaniment and ostinato figures (arco or pizzicato). This removes the danger of a too "soloistic" predominance. In general, we advise against using such demanding instruments, which, after all, only a few students can play. They cannot be appreciated fully for their own characteristic value, and therefore can easily give the players the wrong idea both of the concerns of the *Orff-Schulwerk* and of the duties of a solo instrument. One could say, somewhat paradoxically, that it is more in the interest of violin or piano pedagogy *not* to use these instruments in making music with the *Orff-Schulwerk.* The general awakening of rhythmical and elementary musical strengths that comes from ensemble playing will also benefit every individual study, no matter what type, and it should not be impaired by the mixture and collision of separate areas of interest.

We repeat here what we emphasized initially: *Orff-Schulwerk* is not in any way intended to interfere with solo instrumental training for gifted students or to replace other instruments for music-making. Just the opposite is true: its purpose is to communicate a fundamental musical education to all children, both before and during the time they develop stylistic preferences or undertake special musical training, an education that does not exhaust itself in rote learning of a few songs and a few facts of music theory. For this reason it is necessary to restrict tonal and sound ranges at first to encourage the children to be free and to experiment with their personal creative capabilities. We will now review the step-wise order of this natural musical realm as it is presented in the tools we have at hand, the volumes of printed materials of the *Orff-Schulwerk: Music for Children,* and also offer some methodological advice to help the teacher prepare to use it.

THE FIRST MUSIC LESSONS

Arranging the instruments and music-makers in a group

The instruments are placed according to the same layout as the voice-grouping of a choir, with the deeper voices to the right of the leader and the higher voices to his left. The small percussion instruments may be positioned according to their role in a certain piece. Instruments of similar type are grouped together. Other arrangements may be appropriate for certain activities. When we introduced stamping and clapping earlier we stressed the necessity of flexible grouping, so every individual has enough freedom to move about. The children should learn to arrange and prepare the instruments by themselves from the very beginning, especially "building" the bar instruments, breaking them down, and putting them away, so that they become familiar with the "tools" in every situation. They can learn to line up the tone bars easily, because each bar has its name marked on it. This gives them familiarity with the names of the tones of the diatonic scale practically without help from the teacher. Small children and beginners can arrange the bars according to their graduated size. For work in the pentatonic, bars F and B are removed from C-major. When these preparations are completed we will develop a simple two-note melody ("call") with instrumental accompaniment.

Developing the "call"

It is important that the children actively create their first musical pieces and not learn them by rote. From the beginning they should each have a feeling of creative participation in the musical activities. The teacher cannot be unprepared if this is to succeed. Nothing requires more meticulous preparation than guiding and supervising lessons in discovery and improvisation! More clearly stated: Nothing may be *less* improvised *by the teacher* than lessons in improvisation with children! The teacher's primary task in preparation is to find successful ways and means through which to stimulate the children's individual awareness and discovery of elementary musical prodecures. One important aid is restricting the tonal means to the pentatonic, and within this, to the "call formula." Some two-note "calls" are printed in Vol. I, p. 3 ("Cuckoo" and others), which are then expanded into a little "call melody" in the songs "Rain, rain go away" (H) and "Tinker, tailor" (M). But this does not fulfill our goal of having the children themselves be productive. So we let the children discover the "call-pattern" themselves. There are many ways to encourage this. For example, the teacher can ask a question about the cry of the cuckoo bird, which the children may answer musically both with their voices and with the bar instruments. Some sing the answer; others play. The teacher can use this opportunity to explain to the children how to hold the beaters correctly and strike the instruments. Then it is possible to sing the cuckoo's call at two different levels of pitch. The children can discover these two levels by finding the two open spaces on the bar instruments and playing the bars on either side of them: c-a and e-g, both intervals of a minor third. Singers will get good practice in correct intonation from listening and singing tones or motives that are played on the bar instruments. This kind of imitative singing is far more instructive than imitating another sung tone, because it requires translating instrumental sound into vocal sound. Another way to help the children arrive at the "call formula" is to make use of situations where it occurs naturally: for instance, in shouting or calling across great distances. Short calling words will work ("Hello!" "Help!") as will individual names and short questions ("Where are you?" "Who's over there?"). Children enjoy making up their own words and phrases if they are encouraged to do so. If it is possible, a trip outdoors offers a good opportunity to divide the children into groups across a great distance, so they must make a musical call to be heard.

In these and similar ways the "call formula" is now given down-beat and up-beat structure. Upbeat names ("Maria," "Sebastian") are often sung spontaneously from the fundamental tone upward (presumably the pattern of the "primitive chant"):

Ma - ri-a!

Once the first melody has been created in this manner (through intoning little sayings or verses following the examples in "Rain, rain go away" and "Tinker, tailor"), the children can create a rhythmic accompaniment by clapping, stamping, and knee-patting ("patschen"). Remember everything we have mentioned about the correct ways to clap and stamp. We teach soft (*piano*) clapping by having the children whisper the text in their clearest diction while they stamp and clap softly. The resulting effect must be so distinct that a child standing away from the group can understand every word.

Speech exercises
We introduce the spoken exercise as one of the most basic elements of the *Orff-Schulwerk*. It accompanies all musical exercises, and is itself a musical exercise in the deepest sense of the word. In Vol. I, p. 3 we find some examples of rhythmic accompaniment to be followed one by one and also in combinations of different rhythm patterns at the same time. The simple four-beats of the first line are now set so that a two-part song form is developed.

Starting with simple clapping, we gradually introduce richer subdivided figures and practice them alternately by stamping and clapping. The printed examples are meant to serve only as inspiration for one's own patterns. The teacher should make himself independent of the notated examples, which he can study at home to get ideas for other patterns. With the children he must freely adapt and practice the examples. Accompaniment rhythms are introduced by means of corresponding words, such as those found in the speech patterns, (H: Vol. I, p. 66 ff: "Bluebird" etc.) and (M: Vol. I, p. 50 ff: "Pear tree" "Apple tree" etc.). Speech exercises serve not only a rhythmic purpose, but also help build the voice. Through clear articulation they lead to correct vocal placement and, thus, to optimal resonance. They prevent coarse and throaty speaking and singing.

All the speech exercises should be used at several levels of pitch, in various registers (falsetto, humming, whispering, nasal voice, etc.) and at all dynamic levels. Here, too, the verbal examples are only models and encouragement for finding one's own words, sayings, and sentences to make the characteristic musical-tonal quality of the language sound. We teach basic patterns for subdividing a beat through appropriate spoken words whose syllables describe specific beat subdivisions. First, the whole group pronounces the words together for the whole verse. When that has been well-established, the different words are assigned to smaller groups. These groups pronounce their words simultaneously so the result is "complementary rhythm."

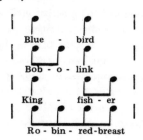

Blue - bird
Bob - o - link
King - fish - er
Ro - bin - red-breast

Next, these rhythms are clapped and stamped while they are spoken. Finally, the children clap or stamp them without speaking them aloud. It is important to redistribute the rhythms among the children often to make sure that every child can perform each rhythmic pattern.

Transfering rhythms to small percussion instruments

After the children have learned to subdivide beats and perform accompaniment rhythms by speaking, clapping, stamping, and knee-patting ("patschen"), (perhaps also using finger-snapping, depending on their individual ability: this sound can enrich our still-primitive palette of sounds), they can begin to transfer these same rhythms to some of the instruments. They will understand the rhythmic figures to be played immediately because they are associated with the words they learned earlier. "The woodblock says 'Blue-bird'." "The rattle now plays the 'King' part of 'Kingfisher'." These and similar instructions spare the teacher the need for complicated explanations or demonstrations of a rhythmic figure. Now there is no need to count out the beat before or during playing, because the living rhythm of speech accomplishes the same goal without the danger of "mechanizing" the children's sense of rhythm. Syncopated patterns present no problem if, for example, the player of the figure "Bob-o-link" is instructed to think the "Bob-o" and play only the "link." The child will sense the first half of the beat (or he may speak it softly to himself) and learn the essence of syncopation naturally, i.e. to place emphasis on the "light" part of a beat and be silent on the "heavy" part. The principle of being silent during a portion of a beat once played, may be extended to the areas of form and macro-rhythm, to remaining silent during larger sections, for example a "tacet" for a group of instruments or a single instrument during a complete formal section. Where, for example, a triangle earlier sounded to mark the beginning of every beat, it may later be restricted to play only at the beginning of a section. If the player has once played his rhythm throughout the section, he will continue to participate in the on-going rhythm internally, keeping the tempo regular and sounding it out loud only at certain places. Long rests are then not "vacations," but "rhythmic silences," during which the child does not set aside his feeling of musical pulse, but keeps it alive internally.

At first it will be difficult for the children to maintain a steady tempo. Letting them take turns conducting the group helps prevent part or all of the group from "running away" or lagging behind the desired tempo.

Introducing the bar instruments

The bar instruments may be introduced into the accompaniment at the same time as the small percussion instruments if the children are instructed to play the bars corresponding to the fundamental tone and the fifth of the appropriate key. The melody the children have already created and played ("call-formula") is played by other instruments. A continuous bass accompaniment using the interval of a fifth is called a *bordun* (drone). The bordun constitutes the simplest tonal support for every pentatonic melody. Its calmness and continuity provide a balance to the movement of the melody. It can stimulate and awaken a melody. For this reason we use it as the basis for all exercises in improvisation. Out of the simplest bordun evolve a rhythmically figured bordun and the "swinging" bordun. In this "swinging" bordun the interval of the fifth is set in motion in steps or small leaps upward and downward on the instrument. Later, more tones can be added to create ornamental figures, or both tones of the fifth can move in opposition or parallel to one another ornamentally. However, because it is the bearer of the basic elementary harmony of the piece, the sound of the fifth must be heard through all the ornamental playing. Examples of the various types of borduns are found in H: I, 76 "Melodic Ostinato" and M: I, 82 "Ostinato exercises for tuned percussion instruments." The first examples are in even rhythm, the later ones in uneven rhythm.

When ornamentation and movement have expanded into independent figures we are no longer speaking of a *"bordun,"* but of a *"basso ostinato,"* in brief: *"ostinato."** The transition from bordun to ostinato is smooth and continuous; therefore, there is no clear distinction between the two. In an ostinato the fifth need not always recur. It can be replaced by its complementary interval, the fourth. (For example, in M: I, ·exercises 23, 24, 27, 67, and others, pp. 82 ff.)

For early accompaniment figures we choose simple borduns whose tones describe the fifth and whose rhythmic pattern is introduced once again through words ("pear tree" "apple tree" etc.). Richer figures should only be attempted when this first assignment has been thoroughly conquered and carried out in ensemble playing without any difficulty or tempo disturbance.

An example of a richer accompaniment figure is found in M: I, 4, in the xylophone notation of piece 3b. All variations may also be played simultaneously. Piece 3c, presents a further increase in difficulty with octave leaps in the alto glockenspiel part and two-note chords in the alto xylophone part. Among these printed examples lie innumerable possibilities for variation; every printed example can be simplified or embellished. We should mention that tonal "clashes" and parallel movement are not contrary to the style of the pentatonic with its bordun and ostinato accompaniments; instead, they are characteristic of this sort of music and lend it its necessary flavor and intensity. The ear should learn to distinguish refinements and color differences of such musical settings. An ear unable to differentiate will imagine that all pieces in the pentatonic lack intensity and one piece is "just like any other." Everything we have already discussed -- that is, learning a little two-note song and accompanying it with all the available instruments -- may be accomplished in the very first lessons. Larger forms result without any additional complications or demands simply from *repetition* and *omission*. The accompaniment alone can function as an introduction even when no recorder or glockenspiel plays the melody to introduce the piece. When voices enter, the accompaniment can be limited to its most important instruments, so that the whole ensemble can join in later in a closing section, giving a "tutti" sound. Moreover, the form of accompaniment can change from verse to verse (new verse created whenever necessary): one verse may be accompanied only by clapping and stamping by all children not seated at an instrument, the next verse by the bar instruments, another with

---

* *fr. Latin "obstinatus": obstinate, always recurring.*

percussion instruments with non-specific pitch, and so forth in any sequence and combination. In all of these exercises there are new formal functions of the individual instruments and voices to consider, but no new technical problems to solve. Thus, they are perfectly suited to reinforce what has already been learned and to refine the children's sense of musical form. They learn to listen for "catch words" or "catch sounds" to mark the entry of their instrument. Through repetition and constant attention the playing technique for all the instruments will improve.

BEGINNING LESSONS IN IMPROVISATION AND INVENTION

General comments

In the first lessons we kept preparatory exercises to a minimum in order to encourage the children in the pure joy of making music together. Still, we should not forget the importance of what we are doing or ignore the need for fundamental work. Here, as in every other craft, we must affirm this from the start. Thus, in the second or third lesson we introduce longer exercises. If they are presented correctly, the children will enjoy them just as much as they do music-making, which is, after all, their goal. Since music-making grows directly out of improvisation, all exercises in invention and improvisation are preparations for it. The basic requirement for successful improvisation is familiarity with materials and tools. Playing techniques for the bar instruments must be developed to a sufficient degree so that they present no obstacle to free and spontaneous playing within a given range of tones. Until this technical level is reached, we limit improvisation to those instruments the children can play without any hesitation: clapping, stamping, and small percussion instruments, introduced in the order of difficulty they present to the player. This order varies for individuals. In addition to the early rhymes, songs and games found in the first section of Volume I, we use the simpler instrumental pieces for training playing techniques. (H: I, p. 48 ff. and M: I, p. 94 ff.) They can be learned in the same manner we suggested for the first little songs. Once again, the printed instrumental pieces are only meant to be examples and models for one's own musical attempts and solutions. Rhythmic and melodic exercises (H: I, p. 66 ff.; M: I, p. 50 ff.) should follow the basic procedure we have already explained: begin with spoken exercises, proceed to "call formulas," followed by simple borduns, rhythms for echo-clapping, melody-building, creating texts, completion exercises, and, finally, improvisation. Detailed remarks are found at the end of M: Vol. I, concerning improvisation. The teacher should read these thoroughly before starting to work. (Of course, comments in other sections of the volume are important also. These are particularly significant because they contain very necessary pedagogical advice.)

We encountered speech exercises at the very start. Now we expand them into rhythmic sentences and sayings. The spoken canons which are most instructive are those which lead to broader complementary rhythms in two-part speaking: see "Speech Exercises" M: I, p. 50 ff., especially "Let well alone," and "Speech paterns" H: I, p. 66 ff.

Different saying can be combined in the sense of rhythmic polyphony, either spoken or played on the instruments. An example is the down-beat phrase, "Mad as a hatter!" combined with the up-beat phrase, "Let the piper call the tune." The tempo should be regular unless a special effect of increasing or slowing the speed is desired.

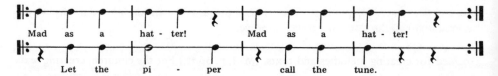

Giving rhythm to certain text

The spoken exercises found in volume I of the *Schulwerk* (H: I, 66; M: I, 50) are early examples of lessons in discovery. The sayings printed there can be given rhythmic life in different ways. Many solutions are possible, and they should all be sought. Every solution must yield a reasonable declamation of the natural rhythm of the words. So the little saying:

> Sunny days
> Funny days
> Shower days
> Flower days
> Cool days
> School days

may be given the following rhythmic treatment (among others):

Sayings of all types (counting-out rhymes, joking verses, etc.) may be given rhythm in this way. When one child has found a solution, all the children should pick up his rhythm and speak the verse after his example. It is possible to sing rhythmical sayings in two and three-note tunes and later in pentatonic melodies. In addition to spoken exercises the children may practice "wordless rhymes" by clapping, stamping, or patting their knees. The words he has spoken earlier will still be active in the child's imagination, although he will only show them rhythmically through the clap, stamp, or knee-pat. Gradually the children will gain familiarity with the elements and means of impro-visation.

Echo-clapping

Echo-clapping is not imitation, but taking up and carrying forward an ongoing rhythm, strengthened by the fundamental technique of construction: *repetition*. No pause or hesitation should occur between the example clapped and the group's response. We recommend that students take turns leading the clapping to prepare themselves for free improvisation. In this exercise ("role exchange") which comes somewhat later the child will provide the first half of a phrase (the "question") and the teacher will "answer," or vice versa.

Creating melodies for given rhythms

In a reversal of the exercise of giving rhythms to certain texts, rhythms are here provided for creating melodies and texts. (M: I, p. 56 ff.) For the children, creating texts will help overcome rhythmic difficulties and offer a lesson in creative language. A few additional remarks must be made about building melodies over given rhythms. The melodic range should not exceed the span of a sixth. For this purpose the extra higher and lower bars are removed form the instrument. On pages 58 and 59 of M: I, we find rhythmic models in uneven beats; complicated rhythms (dotted figures) are introduced. A lovely example for dotted rhythms, accented rests, and asymmetrical periods (groups of three beats) is found in the saying "Christopher, take the mistletoe" on page 59. Thus the richness of rhythmic-metric forms gradually unfolds in alternation with spoken rhythms without any need for the teacher to count aloud or give abstract explanations. Rhythmic ostinato exercises also help develop accompaniments. Examples for such accompaniment rhythms we find in H: I, p. 71 ff. and M: I, p. 60 ff. These examples should stimulate one to his own individual creativity. Improvising above ostinato figures is also a preliminary exercise for playing rhythmic rondos, which we discuss later.

Exercises in completing rhythmic forms

"Completion exercises" can be prepared in the following way: the teacher sings a familiar two-part tune halfway through. The children then complete it from memory. Their completion must be within the general flow of the whole piece. This continuity has been encouraged earlier in echo-clapping and echo-playing. For familiar tunes this question-and-answer game may be done with instruments alone; further, the exchange may take place between groups of children. After this exercise the group may proceed to an informal question-and-answer game introduced with speech exercises. The teacher formulates real questions in a rhythmically spoken tone and individual children answer them appropriately. The text of the answer may be supplied beforehand in order to concentrate the child's attention more on the rhythmic component than on the words.

For example:

This example illustrates two different solutions for the answer. After the children have found their own answers they can learn to distinguish these two forms as two typical varieties of formal two-part structure. The first kind of "answer" (completion) takes up

29

the *opening motive* of the first part and uses it to make the close and complete the form. The second type takes up the *end* of the first half and sets this pattern forth in the last half to close with the "bow" form. Settings can be made double this length, each four beats long, using these two ways of opening and closing the form. The structure of the first half will support one or the other of these alternatives, if it has either a very plastic opening motive, which lends itself to repetition or variation in the second half, or if it has a very open and flowing rhythm, which propels to an unquestionable close. In many cases both types are possible; in this case the interpretation of the first half is left up to the person improvising. The teacher can gain insight here to differences among the children in their ability to grasp these structures.

In these first little forms we can already see the basic elements of the large reprise, chain and "spun out" forms. It is important to practice both types of completion with all the children, especially if their own character types are starting to emerge. For no special tendency of a child should cause him to be limited to certain tasks. He should be encouraged to conquer the opposite task also and learn to acknowledge its value. Genuine individual "style" will prove and establish itself in any case through confrontations with all new and unfamiliar things.

In reference to two-part form, the question whether there are not other typical possibilities for completing a form, (perhaps continuing with a completely new motive) is answered *no.* To continue with new motives is either to create a polar opposite to the first statement, and thus to leave the piece in consideration still open and in need of completion, or to end up with a form constructed as a pair of absolutely unrelated sections. Both solutions are unsatisfactory, for they do not fulfill the present task: that of completing the form with a second statement. Incorrect completions should be brought to the attention of all the children by asking them to listen closely and comment on the solution. Criticism should not be directed solely to the child who performed the completion. No theoretical discussion is necessary in this case. Rather, the listening practice itself will awaken in the children a feeling for balance. The completion exercise is at the same time an exercise in listening, if it is carried out in the way discussed above. Here, as earlier, we recommend exchanging roles between the teacher and children. The children should take turns supplying the opening statement, which the teacher or another child then answers.

Exercises in completing melodic forms
The completion exercises we suggested earlier, first with texts, and later clapped or played on simple instruments, lead directly to echo and completion exercises on the bar instruments. We have already practiced creating small melodic bow forms by building melodies for given rhythms. Now both rhythmic and melodic lines will be created at the same time in the form of a completion exercise. Initial insecurity can be minimized by limiting the number of tones to be used in the improvised melody. Later the children will be able to set these limits themselves.

It is important not to see some of the children's coincidental departures from the "rule" (shortening or lengthening the second part to contrast with the first, surprise closing on other than the expected tone, etc.) immediately as manifestations of the child's creativity. Such *over*-estimations of children's abilities can lead to a pedagogical "false diagnosis" just as likely as the opposite extreme: lower or "shrunken" evaluation of the child's ability.

The child's first apparent inspirations in improvisation usually have their roots in his initial insecurity or faulty memory: the opening statement played for the child is either partially forgotten or has only a superficial effect on him. The connection to the opening statement is broken and the child starts to "swim" when he tries to create an ending. Genuine and convincing mastery over two, four, and eight-beat symmetry as we met it in "Christopher, take the mistletoe," is not derived from chance and error but from enjoyment in changing rhythms. Another asymmetrical form, which has no vertical accents and not tonal progression related to meter is the freely "gliding" melody. Recitative psalmody of prose texts is an example of this form. These forms can be drawn into the lesson plan later when the children have learned to move easily beyond their present structural knowledge. We must caution them too, against confusing incorrect performance with originality, and mistaking coincidence for inspiration. That we cannot and should not exclude all coincidence, every educator and artist who knows how to make creative use of chance happenings will understand. We do not mean to exclude them, but to use them within the learning process, to seize the opportunity and make something out of it as an idea. With children who have apparently played a scale by pure chance we must notice if they then make use of this figure consciously or break it off and start something new. There is a simple way to establish or challenge the credibility of a created melody or completion: after a short pause the teacher can ask the child to play his motive again. If his repetition succeeds without a mistake, or with a little help, one may assume that almost nothing coincidental was a factor. A further, perhaps more effective, argument against coincidence lies in the *flow of the performance.* If the child plays or sings his melody or completion halfway through in one breath, one can confidently consider it a creative act, if he is not copying another child. Naturally the opposite is not always true. Neither the inability to repeat something created, nor a hesitating and touchy performance of a melody, necessarily indicate coincidence or inability. By these methods of proof we can only discern approximately how much the child is aware of his own ability or performance. Far more important an indication of success is the pleasure of all the children and the teacher in the emergence of new tunes and turns. If something lovely and singable results, the question about how coincidental its creation was is no longer as important. In addition to instrumental completion exercises we begin exercises in vocal improvisation. Here the children first give rhythms to certain texts and then intone them.

FURTHER LESSONS IN INVENTION
PLAYING RONDOS

Improvising closed forms

After exercises in completing rhythmic and melodic forms, we suggest inventing and improvising entire melodic phrases or rhythmic forms. The children now have the task to put several "questions" and "answers" together, one after the other, to create a piece which they can perform independently. The solution to the assignment may be vocal (sung or hummed) or instrumental (using bar instruments, recorders, or other melodic instruments), always over a soft bordun accompaniment. Pure rhythmic improvisation on percussion instruments without specific pitch can function as a preparatory exercise for rhythmic-melodic improvisation or as an independent musical task of unique character. How powerful the effect of purely rhythmical values can be, we see in the spoken pieces "The Campbells are coming", The grand old Duke of York", and "Oliver Cromwell" (M: I, 25-27). These texts have no melodic settings. Their unique value lies in the effects of vocal color and sound found in the language itself and its rhythmic accompaniment (which may be enriched by percussion instruments).

Playing rhythmic rondos.
Now it is possible to use the children's readiness in improvising formally closed figures of all kinds to play rondos. This is the first example they encounter of a larger musical form with alternation of *themes* (tutti) and *"couplets,"* (episodes improvised by "soloists").

In the smallest possible rondo, the rondo theme (A) recurs three times. We name the episodes B and C, so the small rondo's scheme is ABACA. The rondo form can then be enlarged with additional episodes and subsequent entrances of the rondo theme. The final section of the piece is always the rondo theme.

"Playing rhythmic rondos" lays the foundation for future formal constructions. The children play these rondos by clapping, stamping, knee-patting, and finger-snapping, later also with small percussion. The rondo *theme* can be structured in a two or three-part form, containing a dialogue kind of exchange between two groups in question-and-answer form. Some examples of rhythmic rondos are found in Vol. I. Moreover, the form of the rondo theme can be introduced and established by using spoken exercises ("rhythmatization" of appropriate texts). The couplets are improvised. To assure regularity of tempo and rhythm the improvisation is always caried out above an ostinato accompaniment rhythm, played again at the end of the theme. The improvised couplet enters best after a rest of two to four beats, during which only this accompanying figure is heard. Now the earlier exercises in completion are used to create the couplets for the rondo. First the couplet is a dialogue between the teacher and one child or a group of children, then between child and child, and finally it becomes a "monologue" played by a soloist or soloist group which carries out both question and answer. We can lengthen the couplet form by repeating the period (first and second parts) and then including a middle section. This is best constructed as a double "question"; thus it will be distinguished from the A section, and given a feeling of "suspension." It is followed by a return, the "reprise" of the A section (question-answer) so the result is a three-part form.

The rondo theme always enters *immediately* after the couplet; a gap would diminish the effect of contrast brought by the re-entry of the rondo theme.

Only when the children are at an advanced level is it advisable to try to improvise without formal structure, that is, to allow the person improvising to set his own tempo and length. Here the difficulty lies mainly in creating a convincing ending, i.e. preparing sufficiently for the final entry of the rondo theme. This task is very difficult when melodic and harmonic frameworks have fallen away. It is better to assign it only after carrying out all the exercises in melodic rondo playing, and then to use it first in playing more advanced rhythmic rondos.

Playing melodic rondos

It is possible to construct rhythmic rondos without making any reference to melody or harmony, because rhythm presents the element of time through the media of sound and tone color, without any need for specific pitch. However, a melodic rondo is inconceivable without a rhythmic component. The designation "melodic rondo" serves, therefore, only to distinguish it from the rhythmic rondo, not to indicate a separation of the melodic from the rhythmic elements.

The pentatonic, lacking half-steps, is a suitable framework for playing melodic rondos. Melodies sung or played earlier in the pentatonic may now form the rondo theme. Of course, rondo themes may also be invented by singing an appropriate saying. The theme does not have to be melodically constant. It may also be improvised during the tutti sections over a given rhythm. In this case the only noticeable difference between theme and episode sections is that between tutti and solo, (both are improvised five-tone melodies, or in the case of the tutti, five-tone harmonies). One suggested opening for a lesson: All the instruments play a previously decided rhythm in the pentatonic, using whatever tones they wish. Although every player plays his own melody, the natural result in the ensemble sound is that of rhythmic "pentatonicism," if no single melody pushes into the foreground. One distinction can be gained by giving the different sections different instrumentation, for example, having the metal bar instruments enter for the first time in the second section. Continuity comes from the accompanying rhythms. The episodes can be performed by "soloists" or "soloist groups" who simply play their own melodies again, or perhaps improvise a new one, so that it now is heard alone or made to stand out in a small arrangement. Playing in a dialogue form of exchange will expand the episodes, as it did in the rhythmic rondo. The players themselves should decide how to distribute the various roles, who is to play the question and who the answer.

In addition to the bar instruments all available melody instruments should join in to improvise episodes and play the rondo theme. The players must accustom themselves to the pentatonic and learn to omit the fourth and seventh steps of the chosen scale – a good exercise!

The observant music teacher will not overlook the fact that the different forms of the rondo correspond in outline to the structure of the "concerto grosso," with its characteristic alternation between tutti *("concerto")* and solo *("concertino")*. This relationship should be pointed out to the children after they have learned to create simple reprise forms and rondos, whenever there is an opportunity to do so and at an age level of the children where occupation with musical form and stylistic problems seems appropriate. This relationship can be illustrated with suitable examples from music literature. Whoever plays such forms himself and does some improvisation will also more easily gain access as a listener to the masterworks.

33

MOVING FROM THE PENTATONIC TO SIX AND SEVEN–TONE SCALES

During teacher-training sessions and discussions the question always arises concerning how long one should continue to use the pentatonic. The answer is *at least* one school year, if there are one or two music hours during the week. Longer use is even better. The greatest evil here, as fundamentally in all education, is the teacher's own impatience. This impatience can lead him astray to treating the pentatonic superficially and ultimately cause him to misunderstand its significance and potential completely. As we explained earlier, restricting music-making initially to the pentatonic provides a good astmosphere for genuine creative work, and thereby leads to an understanding of the seven-tone scale that is independent of conventional formulas. Above all, a person should strive to free himself from the concept that major mode melodies only cadence harmonically. The essence of an elementary major melody, closely connected to the Ionic mode among the later church modes, is built from the same pentatonic mode with which the children are already familiar. Here we note that, in Volume I of the *Orff-Schulwerk: (Music for Children),* the pentatonic derives from that form of children's melody, the "call," as it is found in middle Europe. The conditions found in middle Europe are not valid for all cultures, and are therefore just as generally un-binding as are the language and dialect forms of the various texts in the German publication. The foreign-language editions of the *Orff-Schulwerk* include other pentatonic modes either taken from, or corresponding to, their own heritage of folksong and children's songs.

In every case, however, the pentatonic, lacking half-steps, no matter how its form is modally altered, provides the best foundation for initial lessons in improvisation, precisely there where the customary major-minor realm dominates, and the problems associated with its setting and ensemble sound normally preclude group improvisation, at least at the beginning. (Later we will discuss improvisation further in relation to elementary cadence formulas.)

Tones IV and VII are now added to expand the pentatonic to six and seven tones by bridging over the minor third intervals V-III and VIII-VI. Here we consciously emphasize the step-wise character of these two tones. The children will discover this quality long before they find any harmonic function ("secondary leading tone" and "leading tone"). Accordingly, the bordun again forms the basic accompaniment. From the "swinging bordun" step II and later step IV evolve into accompaniments in their own right, and alternate with step I. Volumes II and III contain examples of songs and instrumental pieces in the major (six and seven-tone scales) over both borduns and step-wise accompaniments. When making music in six and seven-tone scales it is always important to continue to refer to the wealth of songs and exercises in the pentatonic. This does not indicate an educational step backwards or even a standstill. Instead, it helps to anchor the music-making process in its most essential elements: rhythm, melody, and harmony. With the child's increasing knowledge and discoveries, new creative possibilities open themselves again in the pentatonic. Repeated references both to it and to six and seven-tone scales are very productive and help one put aside every temptation to fall back into conventional habits.

A new form of accompaniment now emerges: a second voice that moves in thirds and sixths ("Sleep, baby, sleep" H: II, 4-6; M: II, 6-8). This form was not yet possible in the pentatonic. Ostinato figures can now be given richer construction. Along with the introduction of step-wise accompaniment come new exercises in tonal setting, primarily using the triad. Here the pure triads of the scale move in parallel voice-leading. Contrary to the rules of normal voice-leading, which forbid parallel movement, our concern here is the sonorous harmonic unfolding of a single voice. We find this in many elementary forms in both highly developed and primitive cultures at the source of polyphonic music. A lovely example of this type of musical setting is found in a folksong from Gottschee*, "King Herod and the cock." (M: II, 92-93) In improvisation with triads only pure triads should be used, no "diminished" triads. This means that in the major mode the triad over step VII is excluded. Its harmonic tension would disturb the otherwise easy movement of total sound in the accompaniment.

The setting of "King Herod and the cock" further shows one way to gain freedom from parallel movement through using ornamental figures and tied notes. (See the second part of the song.) This removes the danger of one-sided and monotonous parallel movement. One method of setting a piece should never be permitted to become a habit. Despite its sub-dominant element, the second degree of the scale remains strongly connected melodically to the first, to which it always returns. The sixth step brings with it in relation to step I a special kind of different sound, because both triads together (VI plus I) comprise the pentatonic. This characteristic makes it possible to accompany pentatonic melodies with steps I and VI. Major melodies thus accompanied then get a somewhat minor coloration. This can occasionally be used to create an imperceptible transition from the major to the minor diatonic scale. A good example of a melody made "shadowy" by I-VI accompaniment is found under "I lay me down in peace and sleep", (H: III, 29) and "our Saviour for our sins was slain" (M: II, 101). The musical interpretation of the text here is very simple. Finally, different scale degrees played in alternation and also simultaneously produce a dry modal "major" sound and melody which may be called "Ionic" in the sense of the church modes. The Ionic suggest imminent harmonic (diatonic) treatment, but it is possible to keep a melody independent of this by using the devices of the pedal point, parallel motion, and emphasis of the step-wise and not the functional character of the chords, as it would be found in Classical harmony. ("Gloria" H: III, 35; M: II, 107)

INTRODUCING THE DOMINANT

With the introduction of the dominant we begin a new stage in musical practice, which apparently takes us far away from the world of the bordun and step-wise accompaniment. Without a doubt, harmonic elements now come into a predominant position, and the danger of falling backward into conventional musical ways is clear. This danger we encounter only there where the practices we have constantly encouraged in the pentatonic have not been sufficiently carried out. In the preliminary remarks to Volume III (M) Carl Orff wrote: "Practice with the dominant leads to familiar musical ground, nevertheless it is taken for granted that the previous exercises have so developed and established a feeling for style, that it will be possible, particularly in the field of improvisation, to avoid slipping into conventional patterns."

* (Gottschee: a German-speaking part of Yugoslavia)

So the issue is not to avoid the harmonic effect of the dominant or to inhibit it altogether, but to assess this effect as but *one* possibility among many others, not to value it as the only or the higher form of musical accompaniment. Stylistic one-sidedness is not prevented by excluding some stylistic characteristic, (which could be helpful from time to time as a sort of "diet"), but by acknowledging *all* typical possibilities among the rhythmic, melodic, and harmonic resources in the elementary tonal realm. We caution against developing new prejudices. They may be overcome by uncovering the common bases of all styles! Borduns and step-wise accompaniment are not "pre-forms" or early levels of harmonic accompaniment. They are alternative resources to use in combination or exchange with other musical expressions. When the harmonic element dominates, the melodic steps into the background, and vice versa. Rhythm, however, is still the primary substance. It can be influenced by harmonic effects, but not replaced. The dominant's primary effect lies not in its chordal tension but in its intervallic tension, i.e. the tension between the partial and root tones of the fifth. Chords built over these tones can increase or diminish the tension in the fifth intervals of the bass, and enrich the bass progression tonally or harmonically. Early lessons with the dominant should therefore be tonally as economical as possible and focus attention on the fundamental movement of the bass. This must be experienced in opposition to the linear tension of the melody. The assignments and exercises in settings for flute and drums lend themselves particularly to this purpose. They can be prepared by practicing constructing bass figures in a I-V relationship. At this time it is important to repeat, to practice, and to refine correct drum techniques, paying the greatest attention that the two hands divide the voices well between themselves. The same tonic-dominant figures of the drum should be practiced on all instruments with specific pitch, because the principles apply not only to bass settings, but also to harmonic accompaniment using the dominant. The bass tone is not always the harmonic root. (Inversions of the triad!)

An example of an omitted third in a harmony over the roots of the tonic and the dominant is found in the accompaniment to the ballad "The riddling knight" (M: III, 13). Because only the pure harmony of the fifth is employed, a dominant effect occurs only in the elementary drop of the fifth. The "leading tone" is omitted in the accompaniment and retained in the melody. The same omission of the leading tone (the major third of the dominant) we find in the instrumental dances. Later we will not avoid the full effect of the complete dominant chord. This initial restriction to the essentials should highlight here, as everywhere in the *Orff-Schulwerk,* the evolution of all musical procedures from their original sources. How strong the effect of a drop of a fifth can be is best realized when the resolution to the tonic is delayed over a long span of several measures. In "Carillon de Vendome" (M: III, 22) the dominant has a strong effect because of its sparing use. The song is based on a tonic pedal point, and the dominant first appears in the penultimate measure. In contrast, the melody of "A good-night" (M: III, 28) is supported by the dominant, and only after a lengthy suspension is it allowed to fall to the tonic for the first time in the last measure. Still different from these dominant effects, which extend over long melodic phrases, are pieces which have rapid alternation of tonic and dominant, such as "Sur le pont d'Avignon" (M: III, 36). In a second little French song, "En revenant de Versailles" (M: III, 38), tonic and dominant stand in opposition to each other as two different *keys:* they form the harmonic foundations of the two formal sections of the piece. Within each section the central element is the bordun accompaniment.

We introduce the sub-dominant after the dominant. In the progression I-IV the tension relationship is changed. Now the movement is carried out in the direction of the dominant, but only as far as the subdominant, and then (IV-I) back again to the fundamental tone of the dominant interval; that is, the movement is against the attraction of the harmonic point of emphasis, the dominant. In this return to the tonic the weight of the fundamental tone of the dominant must be overcome, while in the case of the dominant (I-V-I) the movement yields to the attraction of the fundamental tone. The final turn IV-I therefore has a drier, more controlled effect than V-I, because here no "fall" is felt, rather the feeling is that of being *"drawn*-to-a-close."* In the progression V-I the particular effect of harmonic attraction is the dominating factor. Both closing effects should be compared and evaluated in their own right. In the middle of a piece the sub-dominant signifies opposing tension to the dominant, and the two used in succession constitute the complete "cadence", IV-V-I. In elementary settings this progression can be prepared through intermediate changes of I-V-I and I-IV-I. "Street song" (M: III, 48) shows this preparation for the complete cadence in its structure where I is inserted several times between IV and V before IV and V appear in direct succession in the second section, measure 5. How little attention was given to the principles of voice leading is seen in the parallel movement of the harmonies above IV and I, which would be strictly forbidden in traditional music theory. We find further examples of the sub-dominant among the songs and instrumental pieces in this section of volume III (M).

A separate chapter is dedicated to making music with *sevenths* and *ninths*. (M: III) These harmonic forms, wide-spread in middle-European folksong in polyphonic "descant singing," are not cadencing dominant chords. They are suspension tones, and do not follow the normal progression of voice leading and resolution. Instead, they move as whole masses of sound.

One of the most beautiful examples of this kind of treatment is the "Sacred Yodelling Song" (M III, 94), cited in its original unaccompanied form Such unaccompanied polyphonic songs should not be forgotten in favor of making music and singing with instruments. The now richer and more refined dominant can take on a rhythmic function as well, as we find in the "Time-change dances." (M: III, 100 103)

It is essential for constructing and, most important, for improvising such settings that tonal progression take precedence over voice leading. The first concern should be to fill out the basic chords (I, IV or V), that change only occasionally, with both harmonic and rhythmic means. Thus, new melodies can be constructed over one stable harmonic structure, or familiar melodies can be used which correspond harmonically to the given melody, (as in the old form, the "Quodlibet"). Improvising over a predetermined harmonic outline may, of course, also be used when playing rondos, a skill to be encouraged and refined in every tonal realm.

MINOR

In the area of modal diatonics the minor quality indicates that the melodic and harmonic progressions are oriented to the interval of the minor third, found in the first five scale steps.

The effect of the minor third, drawn into the realm of the minor triad, means a far-reaching liberation of melodic resources. We prepare for this effect by reviewing the graduated levels of forms of accompaniment in the modal major. Lessons in the minor thus begin once again with the bordun and step-wise movement, and they may be constructed in the same way that similar exercises were built for the major seven-tone scale.

The grouping of all exercises in the minor into distinct volumes of the *Schulwerk* (IV and V) is, (as in all the previously mentioned instances), not a methodological necessity, but a practical way to organize educational material. In overall design the complete structure follows the lines of natural human development, based on our discoveries with children. In middle Europe, at least, the minor melody in children's music occurs relatively late, only after melody in the pentatonic and major modes, insofar as a "children's music" exists at all. In Volume IV we find examples in the "Aeolian" ("natural" minor), "Dorian," and "Phrygian" modes. These modes are different from each other in their relative placement of half-step intervals, more significantly, however, in their musical characters. In the Aeolian mode, the minor quality is expressed most naturally, (the word "natural" is not meant to be a value judgment), because the tones of the tonic minor chord do not make a "diminished" or "augmented" interval with any of the remaining tones of the scale. In the Aeolian, the diatonic minor remains unshaken, the effect, "suspended," therefore open to both the pentatonic and the major diatonic scale. The *Dorian* mode is characterized by its major sixth above the root tone, which forms in turn a tritone (augmented fourth) with the third tone of the tonic minor chord. This disturbance of the minor third in the Dorian harmonic field, however, lends a brightening effect through the major quality of the sub-dominant triad. The Dorian is the "bright" minor. Therefore it is entitled to be a musical expression of joy, even of exuberance, or, when its contents deal with contrasts and polarity between appearances, it can take on a "light-dark" quality. The *Phrygian* mode, characterized by the minor second (half-step) between I and II, giving a leading tone from above, in contrast, is the "dark" minor. Its tritone lies between II and V and disturbs the stability of the tonic fifth. Therefore, it is often used for expressions of suffering and doubt, for example in the famous chorale "Aus tiefer Not schrei ich zu Dir." In volume IV we find many examples of the minor used characteristically to interpret specific textual contents. The open, supra-personal quality of the Aeolian mode is most suitable for "Pray, children, pray," (H: IV, 3-7), "The Cuckoo's fallen to his death," (M: IV, 41), calendar and weather sayings, prayers, and other pieces with similar contents. The expressive quality of the Dorian is found in "Easter Carol," (H: IV. 19), "Joyous Easter Hymn," (M: IV, 57), the pieces for recorders, and the other songs and instrumental pieces. Texts such as "Mother, o Mother, o hear my cry," (H: IV, 31), "Mother, oh Mother, so hungry am I," (M: IV, 76), and "Mary at the Cross," (M: IV, 87) find their musical expression and symbolic strength in the Phrygian mode. Such relationships between the character of a mode and the contents of a text should never be forced into rigid schemes and too sharply honed symbolism. (Our suggestions have nothing at all to do with programmed hermeneutics!) It is clear that completely unequivocal relationships are impossible. The choice of a certain mode also does not guarantee the success of the musical statement, which only form can supply. To rationalize the correlations suggested above would make their fine and deep distinctions coarse and superficial. The students should not overlook these correlations, but they should never hold them for unabandonable dogmas.

From the above advice it follows that very many of the songs, instrumental pieces, and exercises in the minor diatonic scale, including some of the pieces mentioned earlier in Volumes I and II, are not only appropriate sources of music for children of elementary school age, but also for older students, adolescents, and even for adults. Many of the texts appeal to people of all ages. The concept "child" should be interpreted more broadly here than it is in biology. Something more about that will be said later.

SCALE DEGREES IN THE MINOR

There is no need to mention anything new about using the bordun in the minor; the exercises correspond to what has already been mentioned in earlier volumes. Occasionally, in step-wise accompaniment, relationships in the major are inverted in the minor. Thus, the relationship of I to VII in the minor is the inverse of the sequence I and II in the major; I-III in minor corresponds to the pair VI-I in the major. The shift of harmonic emphasis to the side of the minor is decisive. The more "open" suspended quality of the minor inspires one to develop the ostinato more fully. Now we find examples for expanding simple ostinato figures into "sounding ostinatos," which can appropriately be described as "carpets of sound" and "singing ornaments." The ornamental quality of harmonic setting, which should primarily inspire improvisation, is also the basis for musical forms of another essential sort, as they are found in the dynamic "development" forms or "spun-out" forms of the eighteenth and nineteenth centuries. Educating a feeling for form in the sphere of ornamental (static) structures awakens in the individual an understanding for new music as well as the ability to experience very old forms of music in the pentatonic, from highly-developed and primitive cultures, and from the folklore of all times and places.

After the different degrees of the minor scale have been experienced through the ostinato, the scale steps may be arranged and changed freely according to the structure or direction of the melody to accompanied. Examples of this are found under "Three pieces for recorder or other instruments" (H: V, 23) and "Studies in triads" (M: IV, 117), with remarks at the end of the volume (M). By adding "mixtures" (as one would on the organ) of perfect fourths and fifths, an improvised "organum" setting can be developed by moving the parallel voices up and down. Such a setting remains faithful to the basic structural rule of parallel voice-leading. Changing and shifting the order of the voices should not hide this basis or disturb it altogether. Otherwise the danger exists that the stylistic intentions will be misunderstood and misconstrued to be bad voice-leading. Every improvisation should have a specific form and structural basis, which stimultaneously carries in a basic crystallized structural rule all possible forms and all exceptions, embellishments, and variations. The structural rule of organum is parallel voice-leading in perfect octaves, fifths, and fourths, triads, and inverted forms of these intervals. The collective term for all possibles ways of setting a piece in this manner is *monophony*. It emphasizes the functional equality of all voices, which still lack real individual effect and function. This differs from *homophony* (chordal setting to accompany a single melodic voice), and *polyphony* (independent voices differentiated in rhythm and melodic line). Homophony essentially indicates a progression of *sound* ("Klangmelos"). For historic and stylistic references to these techniques see the remarks about "Decorations of the third" in the back of M: Vol. IV. Exercises in the major should always be included in the musical activities, because one will continue to discover new solutions from his recent experiences in the minor that will also apply to the problems of the major.

FREE RECITATION TONE

Along with increasing independence from the root-tone emphasis of the major, one should evaluate the possibility of a rhythm that is freely suspended, independent of vertical metric restriction, and free of accent, as we mentioned earlier. Reciting appropriate texts on a "psalm tone" finds its obvious starting point in the natural rhythm of speech. Some texts suitable for recitation on one tone with occasional melismatic figures for docorative emphasis are found in H: Vol. IV "Saying" (11) and "The Goose Girl" (34), and in M: Vol. IV "The Bridge" (38), "There is no rose of such virtue" (60), and "Two prayers" (61). Here again, the musical form being introduced should be an occasion for one to refer again to the major and the pentatonic tonal realms to apply this new form there. The heavy emphasis in the major on the fundamental, that we mentioned earlier, is overcome in free reciting, because it is no longer needed to give the piece a structural basis. Every hymn-like prose text (for example, the Psalms) can be recited in this way. It is best to encourage individuals to begin the reciting. This should help the group respond with relaxed and accent-free recitation. One should beware of slow tempos, and try to combine phrases and sentences into longer lines, rather than to emphasize single words. The most important caesuras and endings in the text can be highlighted instrumentally by "musical punctuation." The comma, semicolon, question mark, and colon are indicated on the instruments by clear sounds and higher tones (perhaps by the tension of V), and the period and exclamation mark are represented by dark, "heavy" sounds and deeper tones (the resolved sound of the tonic). The reciting tone holds formal sections together. It should not branch out too often into other tones, and it should only change at the end of a section. When the rhythm of the phrase begins to swing out melodically (something which can no longer be called recitation), the reciting tones becomes an axis for more widely ranging melodic gesture. Combining bound and free rhythms by alternating recitation, songs, and instrumental pieces makes possible an abundance of larger forms. When music-making and dancing are combined, the loveliest possibilities evolve. Nursery rhymes and fairy-tale scenes should be a stimulus for creating such forms, (H: IV, 34-35). It is very important to restrict the harmonic means to be used, to prevent "magical" tone color from sinking into "behind-the-scenes" noise. The notated examples are models for such settings. The scenes may expand into larger "pictures" or "acts" and, finally, into entire fairy-tale plays. It need hardly be mentioned that tonal and harmonic material from the earlier volumes should be used. This supplementing of the pentatonic with the minor found in Vol. IV should be paid particular attention. In the *Orff-Schulwerk* an exercise is never "finished" and put aside. The "new" always contains everything learned earlier, so review is always helpful and important.

THE DOMINANT IN THE MINOR

The fifth volume of *Music for Children* contains the dominant in the diatonic minor, new exercises in rhythm and melody, and new spoken exercises. (M) Their correspondence to the basic exercises in Vol. I, whose continuation and extension they are, indicates their significance. The introduction of dominant accompaniment in the minor mode distinguishes itself from analogous practices in the major through the use of the fifth scale degree *without a leading tone*. This is the form of the dominant found in the pure minor, and it rarely occurs in "Classical" minor style. The lack of a leading-tone puts the effect of the dominant back again in the basic intervallic tension of the fifth, which is the true source of all later complex figures and of the sound of leading-tone effect in major harmony. A melody over a dominant which has no leading-tone is free of harmonic control, if not also completely free from harmonic support. In the early examples the effect of the dominant is still veiled and barely distinguishable from the tonic. (M: V, 2-3). The pieces still depend on the bordun. As we determined when discussing the early dominant exercises in the major, the pieces presented for melodic instruments and drums (or other bass instruments) are especially important for experiencing this essential quality of dominant accompaniment that comes from basic intervallic tension. The pendulum stroke I-V should be done both in quick succession and also with wider spacing. Ostinato figures such as those in "Ten short pieces" (M: V, 3) and "Pieces for various instruments" (H: IV, 9) should be devised in as diverse a variety as possible. Melodic phrases improvised over this type of ostinato should extend over longer spaces, in contrast to those over shorter ostinato figures. (See also the remarks about these exercises in the back of M: Vol. V.) These melodies may also be in the Aeolian, Dorian, or Phrygian modes, for the minor dominant is harmonically compatible with each of these three modes. According to the models found in Volume V it is now possible to give the students an assignment to construct simple three-voiced settings using only the tonic and dominant. In this way sayings and proverbs may be given sonorous settings. Even this modest harmonic frame provides enough opportunity for creative achievement. The effect of a major close in the minor realm (see "Winds" M: V, 22) is just as usable as are a minor close, the pure interval of a fifth, or a unison. The students should be encouraged to observe fine differences and various ways to construct a close. For pieces invented by a group it is not necessary to single out one final solution as the "very best." The students should be asked to make their own evaluations. Along with the increasing expansion and enrichment of

41

the tonal and harmonic materials they have at hand, their personal characters will become ever more differentiated through their invention and improvisation exercises. As part of this expanded material we now encounter ballad form, the epic song, in a new treatment. "Herr Olaf" (M: V, 24), is an example of the original form of a ballad, in contrast to the later stylized, through-composed ballad form of the Romantic period which was intended for soloistic performance. The text of "Herr Olaf" is discussed at the back of the volume, along with a translation of the German verses. (M) The original ballad was actually a choral *round dance*. It is especially effective if "Herr Olaf" can be produced and performed in this way, with highly developed and predominant rhythm.

Introducing the Leading Tone in the Minor

It would be an error to want to conclude from the concept of the "harmonic minor" found in the cadencing harmony of Classical and Romantic music, that the leading tone in the minor is restricted to these musical styles. We find the leading tone in countless minor melodies of folklore that, in many cases, certainly have nothing at all to do with Classical music. The leading tone can be significant melodically as well as harmonically, intervallically as well as chordally, accidentally as well as essentially. Therefore, it would be the ultimate in Puritanism not to use it for fear of falling back into restrictive stylistic habits, just as it would not be less one-sided to use it exclusively. Once again it seems necessary to introduce the leading tone with caution at first, clothing it modestly by tonal and chordal means, that is, to emphasize at first its *melodic* function. It is important to include bordun exercises, to improvise simple supporting bass lines to accompany the single-voiced lead melody, and to continue to reintroduce earlier exercises without leading tones, to maintain the children's already well-reinforced relationship to elementary sources. The leading tone can also alternate with the minor seventh interval of the natural minor within a *single* melody. We indicated this earlier in the first example of a minor melody with a leading tone: "Old midsummer melody", (M: V, 29). The seventh step of the natural minor is supported here by a triad built on the third step (the mediant), which given counter-tension to the dominant major triad, and thereby to the harmonic leading tone. This counter-tension is often found in old songs and settings, in the major, too, where the whole step to the tonic (minor seventh to the fundamental tone) contrasts with the major dominant as a "Mixolydian" conceit. The mixolydian step in the major can occur in a major triad (explained in functional theory as the "subdominant of the subdominant") or in a minor triad (minor dominant in the major). In the minor, the minor seventh tone (VII of the modal minor) can appear as the fifth of the triad of the III or as the root tone of the triad of the VII. After the inclusion of the major dominant chord, both of these chords may still occur in the same piece. Modulations into the parallel major key (for example in the middle of the "Catalan Christmas dance" M: V, 36) give formal significance to the tension between the major dominant in the minor key and the fifth of the parallel major, which is at the same time the minor third above the fifth step 'in the minor. In the complete tonal field the succession of leading tone and "stepping" tone (as one could name the seventh step of the modal minor) brings chromatic tension into the diatonic, to which a second kind of tension now enters: the tension between the minor six and the major seventh ("augmented second") in the minor with leading tone. This tension is usually removed by raising with the sixth step of the scale — we prefer to say by the introduction of the Dorian sixth — in the so-called "melodic minor." In this scale the minor quality comes forward only in the minor third found in the tonic triad (third step); therefore, in the descending "melodic minor" scale both the raised sixth and seventh steps are cancelled, so that the natural minor is immediately juxtaposed to the "majored" minor. In the section of remarks in volume V (M) we find examples of different minor tunes and ways to handle a leading tone cited and explained. Complementing this advice, which, as we expressly emphasize in this case, is fundamental in importance, the following should be noted: in addition to the already discussed possibility of introducing the leading tone purely melodically over a bordun, and the other possibility, bringing it into the same harmonic field of a melody or piece next to the "stepping" tone, it can also be fully relieved of dominant function if it is supported by its perfect fifth above, or perfect fourth below, for example, through its minor triad, or (in the case of the upper voice) through a sixth chord. The harmonic effect yields to a tonal one; the leading tone becomes the root of an interval or chord and takes to itself a partial tone that lies outside of the basic tonal field, for example the ending B - D-sharp - G-sharp — a-e-a. (Chords notated from the bottom upward.)

D-sharp is foreign to a-minor, and it blocks the dominant function, which in the Classical minor would be characterized by the dominant seventh "d," from coming into its own. Again we have before us a "dry" tonal melodic turn that frequently occurs as a final expression in organum settings ("fauxbourdon"). See the example of a fauxbourdon under the suggested advice at the end of M: Vol. V. Gothic music, accessible once again today, (the organa of Perotin, music of G. de Machaut, and other masters of the eleventh to thirteenth centuries), provides us with countless examples of the range of stylistic possibilities and individual beauty of such musical forms.

While the liberation of the leading-tone from its dominant function emphasizes the sound rather than the function of the minor second step, its combination with the tone of the minor sixth indicates sharpened *harmonic* tension. However, the interval of the augmented second, in addition to its usual progression in Classical harmony: that of upward movement (leap into the leading-tone followed by normal resolution of leading-tone tension) can also be freed to stand itself as a characteristic interval. As such it acts *against* the tendency of the leading-tone, staying on the tone of the minor sixth, or springing back from this, etc.) without giving way to the tendency of a leading tone from above, (resolution of the minor sixth into the fifth). Here, too, harmonic tensions are suspended or left unresolved in the richer musical textures and decorative melodic turns. The examples from eastern and south-eastern European folklore found at the back of M: Vol. V are representative of many. They may stimulate one to discover and evaluate all the typical ways to use the leading tone in the minor, without sacrificing the modal foundation of the minor diatonic.

The fourth scale degree in the minor; Descant
The introduction of the fourth step (subdominant) in the minor brings with it no new problems. The effect of the "plagal" cadence, fully discussed earlier, becomes even drier

in the minor than in the major because of the quality of the minor triad. The lighter feeling created by using the Dorian sixth (major subdominant in the minor) may now also be supported harmonically. Now that we have discussed the complete fundamental harmony of all music in seven-tone scales, improvisation exercises may take on an expanded form. A new assignment is making "descants" over given melodies or settings (which can be finished pieces within themselves). This exercise is further explained in the remarks in the back of M: Vol. V. Examples are found in M: V, 60. When making descants, one's chief purpose is to add an upper voice to a given melody or harmonic structure. As we recommended for all exercises in improvisation from the very beginning, the improvised line should be spontaneous, and any tendency to stop and improve the line should be avoided. It is better to put up with a melodic slip than to interrupt the rhythm of the line. Of course such slips will eventually become less common. Descanting is possible with all melodic instruments and with the voice without text, either humming or singing. The melody or setting which forms the foundation for the descant must be familiar to the descant-makers before they start to improvise. From descanting a direct path leads to free variation, first developed in the example of the *chaconne.* (M: V, 61) The chaconne is an ostinato form which grows out of earlier ostinato exercises. With it, we have reached the outermost border of the area of elementary music exercises and musical practice handled in the *Orff-Schulwerk.* On the other side of this border begin the areas of harmonic theory and the study of composition.

In the last volume of *Music for Children* rhythmic and melodic exercises and spoken pieces appear once again. (M) They signify a continuation and fulfillment of the exercises started in Vol. I. More complicated structures, such as changing meters, further recitative interpretations of greater length, combinations of spoken texts and instrumental accompaniments, and freer melodic structures are introduced in examples and exercises. These exercises should be combined with materials from the previous volumes. Beyond the rhythmic and melodic exercises it is important for us to hear the relationships between word and sound, word content and music, work rhythm and the tonal realm found in the examples of setting tonally or making rhythmic great poetry, such as the texts from Goethe's *Faust* and that of the chorus from Sophocles' *Antigone.* The same is true for recitative interpretations of the Christmas stories and Easter stories and other texts.

Many examples in the last volume of *Music for Children* give one the opportunity to practice making instrumental settings for certain pieces either with a free construction or with some kind of tonal "registration" as suggested earlier. The only true regulators for good instrumentation are hearing and good taste, well-schooled by good examples; a further regulator is fidelity to the text and the content of the piece to be given instrumentation. Special attention is paid to harmonic balance among equal voices in the piece.

CLOSING CONSIDERATIONS

When we look over the entire *Orff-Schulwerk: Music for Children* discussed here, the abundance of materials printed in the five volumes of exercises, songs, pieces, instrumental works, and assignments may at first shock us; and, to be sure, this wealth is only the remainder of much more comprehensive material that Carl Orff and his associate Gunild Keetman assembled during long years of work. "The *Schulwerk* is a pruned hedge," Carl Orff once remarked during a talk. That worthwhile parts sometimes fell sacrificed to the clippers was unfortunately unavoidable, if the work was to be published in a realizable form today. We had to omit all of the planned-for presentations of possible connections between making music with the *Schulwerk* and play and dance. This will be compensated for in additional single booklets on basic forms of elementary play and movement, tried and developed in the meantime, which correspond to the statement of musical and pedagogical goals of the *Orff-Schulwerk* as far as it is possible to describe and write about these things at all.

The *Orff-Schulwerk* is a beginning that is not in search of a conclusion, but seeks continual alteration and modification, both indicators of life. As such it is not concerned with special methodological and technical problems -- these every educator must solve for himself on the basis of his own experience and with consideration of his professional situation. Rather, it addresses current musical-pedagogical questions of fundamental meaning. A teacher who has recognized the earnestness of these questions will not capitulate after encountering possible difficulties during the first weeks or months of work, only to turn backward into old practices. Instead he will continue his attempt to accustom himself and his students gradually to the light of new freedoms. This light, like that of Plato's "Analogy of the Cave," may sting at first and strike one helpless. The reluctance of the students is often only the result of the teacher's own hesitation. Genuine joy in an assignment communicates itself to everyone who works together.

Music for Children is also music for all people who have not let their childlike natures die, but have preserved them and can reawaken them to be the innermost core of their lives. Not infantile ("childish") impulses, which turn this core into an empty shell, but the realization of the origin of spiritual freedom and personalized lives leads to *homo ludens,* to whom the seriousness of child's play has become the reality of a mature style of life.

The song of Francis of Assisi, one of the purest expressions of a man who has matured into becoming a child of God, stands not coincidentally among the last examples of the *Orff-Schulwerk.*

The entire work ends with the poetic-symbolic quatrain from Goeth's "Walpurgis Night's Dream," whose light innuendo of pessimism should cause one to think and reflect.

> *Orchestra (pianissimo)*
> Wolkenzug und Nebelflor
> Erhellen sich von oben
> Luft im Laub und Wind im Rohr
> Und alles ist zerstoben.*

---

*Floating clouds and mists recede
the shades of night are banished
Morning wind in tree and reed,
and swiftly all has vanished.*

SUGGESTIONS FOR TEACHERS

Preliminary remarks:

The following suggestions are mainly intended to help the teacher prepare and assemble lessons for groups of children, but they will also give him a means for judging how successful he is in his own teaching. The suggestions pertain primarily to the music-educational side of the *Orff-Schulwerk*, but they can also be of use in the area of movement education. This is a compendium of basic "rules of thumb" for teaching. It does require some previous acquaintance with teaching methods. The suggestions should be amplified and altered by the individual. (Some examples have been notated with letters to indicate tones or chordal progressions.) These suggestions all depend on using the volumes of the *Schulwerk*. They supplement this writer's introductory booklet which gave all the necessary information for playing the instruments correctly and making use of the structure of the *Orff-Schulwerk* itself. Here I have limited myself to suggestions based on my own discoveries, observations, and, above all, my own mistakes.

In the left margin of the text the main points of this presentation are noted in short words and phrases, to facilitate quick scanning and easy review of the materials.

BASIC PRINCIPLES

Educational goals

1. It is the main task of the teacher and educator gradually to make himself superfluous. One educational goal has been reached when the student can solve an assignment without help from the teacher or anyone else. An educational step is taken when he *wants* to do this independently. In music education this means that a musical lesson has accomplished its goal if it has awakened in the student the desire to continue and repeat the exercise outside the class period.

Group: individuals playing together, not a "collective"

2. A musical group is not a collective. It should be seen as individuals playing together. In every class period each student must be encouraged personally to assume a task in the group's music-making and to feel he has been successful.

Circular seating arrangement

3. We recommend that the musical group be arranged in a circle, instead of having all the children face forward. The circle can also be "pear-shaped" with the teacher sitting at the point of the "pear," or perhpas a three-quarter circle will allow him to observe the group more closely.

Proper seating

4. The children should sit on stools or cubes with a flat surface, if possible anatomically designed. They must be able to reach the floor easily with their feet. Turn a square seat so that the child sits across a corner. Each person must have enough freedom of movement and "elbow room."

Clothing

5. Sport dress is indispensable for both the children and the teacher. Gym shoes, or, when temperature and floor conditions allow, bare feet are appropriate for dancing and making music. *Never* use stocking feet, because of the danger of slipping.

Arranging the instruments

6. Have all the necessary instruments arranged before the class begins, if possible. Place the bar instruments at correct height: knee-level for seated players, waist-high for those standing. Seated players are close to the instruments; standing players are not as near. Have a soft pad ready to hold the small percussion instruments.

Sitting, standing, moving.

7. Do not spend the whole period seated, standing, or in constant movement. The best arrangement is to alternate these three possibilities during the hour according to the lesson plan. The teacher should sit, stand, and move along with the group.

Recess

Better twenty minutes
daily than 2x weekly
sixty minutes, or one
time of 120 minutes

8. If the teacher is forced to spend longer than 45 minutes in music and movement teaching, he must include a long intermission at this time (5 to 10 minutes), and afterward change activities. If he can decide for himself how to apportion the time (in the kindergarten and early elementary grades), the optimum plan is to spend 20 to 30 minutes daily for elementary music and movement lessons, rather than having two sixty-minute periods a week, or one whole hour or double-hour once a week. In addition to the music hours in the curriculum the teacher can in good conscience make use of physical education periods, divide them into daily segments, and devote them to movement education lessons. Within every lesson period there should be at least one short "breathing and relaxing" time when the children may lie relaxed on their backs for a few moments.

Not director, but
guiding player and
helper

Role exchange

9. The teacher should be only "primus inter pares", (one among equals), that is, *not* a director and commander, but a guiding participant and helper. In every lesson some children (not always the same ones) should exchange places with the teacher ("role exchange") and lead the group.

Purposeful and
well-founded praise

10. Give praise for good performance, singling out the child by name. ("You are holding the beater just right" is better and more effective than merely, "good".)

Do not criticize;
help and correct

11. Do not criticize or punish unsatisfactory performance, but improve upon it through repetition and helpful suggestions. ("That was already quite good. Now try it again and this time watch to be sure you are also playing with your left hand".)

Supervision and
correction; individual
supervision without
singling out one child

Observing the
group

12. Next to instruction, the most important task of the teacher is to supervise the children's performance. This calls for praise or correction immediately after the first lesson. Continual supervision will make it absolutely unnecessarry to hold perfunctory and evil examinations at specific intervals. Monitor the children individually as often as possible, but never single out one child to criticize or make nervous. During singing and playing walk softly around the circle, listen carefully, and observe how and what the children do.

What and how

13. Not only what, but also how music is made (spoken, played, and danced) should be watched, constantly supervised, and corrected. Never be satisfied with rote memory exercises (texts, songs, or instrumental parts

learned "by heart"), but consider the quality of the performance even during the lessons to be very important.

14. When teaching spoken pieces or songs, speak and sing very clearly for the children. (See the suggestions for method below.) Later, however, speak and sing as little as possible with them; instead, listen very carefully!

Demonstrate clearly but do not always sing along

15. If, in spite of repeated friendly warnings, disciplinary difficulties do arise, (individual disturbances, spitefulness, nonsense, wrong use of the instruments), do not handle it by screaming or otherwise causing the children to be afraid. Rather, point out to the disturbing child that if he repeats his act he will be removed from the group. If the whole group is disrupted and upset, either introduce an intermission or catch their attention by offering challenges. ("Who can get absolutely quiet the fastest?" or, "You may talk to each other now as much as you want, and when you hear the drum, be quiet," etc.) Whoever reacts well to this challenge may receive an instrument to play. (In large disturbances, place the instruments together in the middle of the group. The quietest possible putting down the instruments may also be practiced with a contest.) Rewards are more effective than punishment! (Corporal punishment is criminal treatment of a child, as is cynical taunting, which can injure him even more than bodily punishment.)

Disciplinary difficulties; do not shout; instead use reasonable measures

Challenge-type discipline exercises

Reward more effective than punishment

METHODS FOR SPECIFIC EXERCISES
A.   EXERCISES IN INTERPRETATION

I. SPEECH EXERCISES:
Goals

These exercises improve rhythm and voice-training, and help develop awareness of language.
Procedure:
1. Pronounce the text with good articulation and rhythm.

2. Have the children repeat it in stages, always beginning at the top and adding lines gradually.

3. Correct mistakes immediately! Help the children, but do not always speak the text with them. If some cannot repeat the text, or have trouble with some words, let other children volunteer to help.

Correct immediately! Let individuals speak and help

49

Dynamic, tempo and register variations

4. Make use of every repetition necessary to practice variations in dynamic range (loud, soft, very soft, crescendo, diminuendo), vocal register (normal voice, head tone, falsetto, humming, whispering, nasal tone), tempo (normal, slow, very slow, fast, very fast, accelerando, ritardando). The children thus discover and practice several means of interpretation while they are learning the text.

Canon

5. Have the children speak in canon and experiment with different orders and times of entry. (Once again, use different vocal registers.)

Vowels, syllables, animal sounds

6. Speak the rhythm of the text in syllables and sounds for voice-training (vowels, certain voiced consonants, diphthongs, etc.). For children, translate the text into "animal talk": cow, frog, sheep, bee, pig, etc.

Sounding gestures for text rhythm

7. Have the children produce the rhythm pattern of the text by clapping, knee-patting, stamping, and finger-snapping.

8. Construct accompaniments from sonorous words of the text. Individual children may recite the entire text while the rest of the group performs the accompaniment.

II. SINGING EXERCISES:

Learning a song

Procedure:

Presenting the song

1. The teacher sings the whole song for the children, smoothly and with careful and clear attention to the text and intonation.

Learning the text

2. Speak the text together in the rhythm of the song. (See speech exercises)

Learn melody in sections

3. Sing the melody in sections to the children and have them sing it back by themselves. The teacher should not sing with them, but watch carefully and enter only when it is necessary. (Sing only the missing tones, motives, or words very softly.) To learn additional lines, always start from the beginning of the song; never begin in the middle.

Dynamics, tempo, transposing

4. Vary dynamics and tempo. Transpose the melody into different but reasonable keys.

5. Sing and hum the melody without the text in voice-building syllables (me, may, mah, mo, moo, etc.) or with certain voiced consonants (Mmm, Nnn, Zzz, Ng, etc.). Or imitate animal sounds (see Speech exercises, 6).

Where to breathe
Breathing exercises

6. Decide on where to breathe in the song. Introduce breathing exercises. (These may also come between 2. and 3.)

Some sing, others
keep rhythm

7. Individual children or groups can sing alone while the others keep the rhythm.

Conducting exercises

8. Individual children take over directing the group and trade places with the teacher. Eventually everyone should have conducting experience.

9. Practice a perfect unison attact, signalled by the director's breathing precisely in and out, or by a clapped introduction, if the children have not yet learned the appropriate conducting patterns.

Singing with hand
signals and syllables

Describing the
melodic contour
in the air

10. Sing the melody in solfege syllables (tonic "do") with the corresponding hand signals. (The teacher demonstrates with two hands; the children follow.) If the syllables and hand signs are not yet familiar, or are completely new, indicate merely the contour of the melody in the air with the right hand, or both hands. If the children are already fluent with syllables and hand signs these may be used in learning the melody.

Transfering the
melody to instruments
Singing absolute
pitch names

11. Assuming sufficient technical playing ability, some students can try to play the melody by ear on an instrument (recorder, bar instrument). The other children can sing along, using the names of the absolute pitches if these are already familiar. If the song is simple, it is possible to use this occasion to introduce the absolute pitch names. (If the melody is only sung, the tone names do not have to comply to the absolute pitch of the key sung, but may refer to a simpler key with only a few accidentals.) In any case whenever the instruments are used the correct names must be sung.

Let the children sing
and conduct the song;
at the end sing it
again with the text

12. At the end of the lesson have the children sing the song with text again themselves while one child directs the group. The teacher should sit in the circle and observe the result.

III. INSTRUMENTAL EXERCISES:

When a piece is to be played with Orff instruments and small percussion instruments, or a song is to be accompanied with instruments, the following rules should be observed in addition to the above mentioned suggestions:

Everyone practices every part! Imitate instruments by clapping (percussion) and syllables (bar instruments and recorders)

1. Practice each individual part with the *whole group.* Even children not sitting at an instrument participate by clapping or singing, or using a syllable to approximate the sound of the instruments: ("Ploom" for xylophone, "Cling" for glockenspiel, "Too" for recorder.) Only when *all* the children have practiced *all* of the voices, should the parts be distributed to individuals and smaller groups.

Partners — so non-players learn part by watching

2. Children who are not occupied when the piece is performed should be given a partner who is playing and try to learn his part by watching carefully. The child can raise his hand when he feels he can play the part and then changes places with his partner. This way all the children are occupied with the instruments.

Conducting practice

3. Instrumental pieces offer good opportunity for practicing conducting. A child may take over the teacher's part at the end of a lesson and direct the group. Always let the children make music by themselves at the end of the lesson!

B.   EXERCISES IN IMPROVISATION

I. PLAYING RHYTHMIC ECHOES:

Procedure:

Tempo

1. Explain and locate the pulses of the children in the group. Then have everyone tap softly with his toes or pat his knees until a unison tempo is reached which approximates the average pulse rate of the group.

Explain the assignment

2. The teacher explains what tempo will be used and how he will indicate it (for example by clapping, knee-patting, finger-snapping, or a combination of these). At first the best is a motive of two measures of 2/4. (A quarter beat equalling a medium pulse, about 70-80 per minute.)

Change dynamics and
color
Group answers in an
echo

3. Encourage the group to imitate the sample motive in the same tempo without hesitating or interrupting the continuity. The teacher may change both dynamics and tone color by clapping in different ways: with hands cupped or held flat. He can also change the motive itself if he keeps the time structure the same, and checks to be sure the change is heard and reproduced by the children.

Individuals take
turns, first in a
series, than in
surprise turns.

a) When the whole group has performed the echo successfully, individual children may do it. First one follows the other in turn. Later the order is unspecified, and the teacher may indicate with a nod of his head who is to be next.

b) Then follows "exchange of roles": each child receives a turn to clap an example and indicate who is to be his "echo partner." This child may complete the echo and give a new pattern to be echoed by another student. Thus a "chain" game evolves, and we have introduced improvisation. (It lies in the assignment to clap a new pattern spontaneously.) *Important!* The whole group should clap an accompaniment motive softly while the soloist is responding.

New task:
vary tone but
keep same rhythmic
structure

4. New activity: One child may clap a *rhythmic* motive. Another child echoes the motive but with a *different sound*. For example, a *clapped* motive may be echoed by *knee-patting,* finger-snapping, or any combination of sounds, as long as *the rhythmic pattern remains the same.*

5. Activities 3 and 4 can be altered and made increasingly more difficult by *changing the rhythm* (triples, complex beat patterns of four and six beats, then five beats, changing beats within a pattern, etc.); *lengthening the figure* (four-beat groups, three or six beat groups, each discussed beforehand); or *changing the phrasing* (introducing upbeat motives).

II. EXERCISES IN COMPLETING RHYTHMIC FORMS

Procedure:

1. Explain and establish a tempo (see I, 1.). Give an example of question-answer form and demonstrate the effect of finality by using appropriate texts:

and answer (Texts) Final effect *("Rose")*	"Mother may I go with Peter to the park to play? "No, my dear. Stay right here. Wait for another day." or: "Dandelion, dandelion, iris, buttercup Dandelion, dandelion, iris, *rose*."
Four two-beat, or two four-beat groups for an opening statement	The best opening sentence (the "question") is constructed as a group of four two-beat or two four-beat groups. (tempo: quarter = 70-80) Now encourage the children to pick up the sample motives as it is clapped, and then try to create a feeling of finality, so the final word ends on the stressed part of the last beat. *("rosé")* Avoid making the last beat of the *opening* statement feel "final." Do not forget the suggestions under I: 3, 4, 5, (exchanging roles) in carrying out this lesson.

Two ways to complete
rhythmic form
	2. There are two ways the "answer" can be related motivically to the "question."
	  a) Using the *opening motive*
	  b) Using the *final motive* ("spinning out" the form)
	
	Method (a) produces a two-part formal structure where the answer is more strongly related to the question. Method (b) produces a more "bowed" form with an apex. Both possibilities are *equal in value*, even though an opening statement will sometimes seem to call for one kind of answer rather than the other.

Dialogue to monologue (each answers himself) Rondos from alternating tutti and solo	3. After all the children have improvised both question and answer, they should do both by themselves. That is, they now answer themselves. (The transition here is from dialogue to monologue, or from an exercise in completing rhythmic forms to an exercise in "inventing.") This is best begun in the group, and only later carried out "soloistically." From a sequence of tutti (all children play their figures at the same time) and solo ("soloistic" groups entering) the form of the *rondo* is gradually developed.
Expanding the form by repeating the period	4. Develop this exercise one step further by expanding the form through *repetition*. Here a period, consisting of a question and an answer, may be repeated. (A good memory exercise!) Improvised sections should also be repeated, the "question" as well as the "answer." The answer may be varied by using a decisive "closing formula" in place of a repetition.

5. Vary the periods internally by using different basic rhythms, upbeat phrasing, syncopation, and other rhythmical structures.

Internal variation

6. Breaking through the symmetry of the period: through echo-type "added motives" ("Coda" at the end). This is most simply achieved by repeating *(p)* the last two measures of the opening statement and final statement, or only the final statement. (Example out of the literature: the opening theme of the great C major symphony of F. Schubert.)

Breaking through the symmetry of the period by adding motives

7. Expand the form by including a middle section ("B") after the first period ("A") is repeated. This is best constructed in the form of a complex "question-question" (eg. opening statement plus echo). This corresponds to exercise I, with a four-beat introduction and an echo. It contrasts in dynamics and tone with section "A". After "B," section "A" recurs as a reprise, and is not repeated. In review: A and B are improvised. A is then repeated, followed by the second part of B (as an echo), then A as a reprise after B. This requires good memory and is a good exercise. The result is the classic reprise form AABA.

Expanding form to reprise AABA

"B" is not question-answer, but question-question. (e.g. statement-echo)

8. The reprise form AABA may form the basis of a rondo, used both in the theme and as a framework for the episodes. (Couplets)

Reprise as basis for rondo theme and couplets

9. Other types of form can be developed out of the elements A and B in addition to the reprise form AABA: Bar form AAB, counter-bar form ABB, variations $AA_1A_2A_3$, etc. One need only alternate the contents of the formal elements. This is true for all complex structures, even the reprise form, which can itself be altered. Other forms are the rondo types ABABA and, through the introduction of a C section, ABACABA.

Evolving other formal types: AAB, ABB, $AA_1A_2A_3$, ABABA, ABACABA

10. Aperiodic time structures can be developed from the dialogue without being bound to classical metrical and periodic systems. The first step is a "rhythmic conversation" with free motivic construction (avoiding two and four-beat groupings which only lead back to symmetry), and unspecified length (very short statements are allowed, as they are found in a real conversation). The only "rule" needed is that each

Aperiodic time-structures in free dialogues

conversational partner always allow himself to be interrupted. He should stop whenever his partner makes it known that he wishes to "say something." Continual talking at the same time is also allowed. The goal should be a balanced exchange between "speech" and "counter-speech" with a convincing final ending. This method of dialogue may also be built into the rondo form as a way of creating couplets

Synthesis of aperiodic rhythmics and formal structure through mensurated motivic structures

11. A synthesis of aperiodic rhythmics and formal structures can be reached by building motives out of "mensurated time references." In this example, tones are related to one another, but their lengths are not determined by beats, but by counting in the smallest possible subdivision of time. The group accompanies with a neutral eight-beat without any accent or feeling of downbeat, while the person improvising claps a figure without beat-reference but strictly bound to the value of the eighth, which gives the basic measure. This improvised figure constitutes a formal section which may either be added to or closed by another person improvising. Because the formal sections here are not regulated in their length, as they are in periodic structure, it is necessary to arrange a signal to indicate when the partner should begin his section. He may enter according to his own feeling, whenever he believes he is able to continue successfully, at which time the first person stops.

III. RHYTHMIC POLYPHONY

Procedure:

Building a polyphonic ostinato by adding motives

"Liberating" the ostinato at the end of construction

1. One student improvises a two-beat ostinato. His motive must extend over two beats; a repeated one-beat motive does not constitute a two-beat ostinato! While he continues to perform his ostinato, his neighbor adds a contrasting ostinato motive and continues with this. The next person adds another motive, and so on, and all persons continue their own ostinati. Differences in sound should also be used, as far as the still limited means allow. When the last person has had his turn, the ostinato motive may be "liberated." That is, when a leader has given a sign, the ostinato is abandoned and the group improvises a rhythmic form over the basic tempo and meter. (Length is always variable. Each student should strive for clarity of form.) The piece is ended when the last person has reached the end.

2. Enlarge upon exercise 1. by using a "Chaconne": in place of the two-beat motive, the groups evolve a four or eight-beat theme. One group continues to repeat this theme. The others add several new layers of voices above by gradually adding complementary motivic structures one after the other, until all individual have entered and a full sound is reached. This can then be "unbuilt" in a similar way until only the original theme remains. (Of course the piece may also end at the climax when all voices have entered.)

Complementary
rhythms

3. Improvise complementary accompaniment figures for the forms developed above in exercises I and II. (Take this opportunity to repeat these earlier exercises.)

Accompaniment for
spoken pieces and
songs

4. Improvise forms of rhythmic accompaniment for pieces to be sung or spoken. (See the suggestions for singing and speaking exercises.)

Introducing small percussion instruments
All the exercises under I, II, and III have been carried out with the "natural" instruments (hands, feet, fingers, thighs). They can be used analogously with small percussion instruments. Pay attention to a balanced use of all of these resources, to correct playing techniques, and production of the various possible tone colors. Experiment with all variations of beat, tone, and dynamic range. No new methodological problems arise

Small percussion

with the exercises themselves when small percussion is introduced, as long as only instruments with unspecified pitch are used. All the instruments should have only rhythmic and color functions.

IV. MELODIC IMPROVISATION

*1. Creating melodies for given texts, rhythms, and forms.
(Vocal and instrumental)*
   a) unrestricted use of tones
   b) specified, or limited tonal range

Construction progresses in two directions:
   1) increasing complexity of rhythmic pattern
   2) increasing complexity of tonal structure

Procedure:

Speak saying in
rhythm

a)1 The group speaks a saying rhythmically in full duple meter. (See speech exercises) "Peter, Peter, pumpkin

57

eater, had a wife and couldn't keep her; Put her in a pumpkin shell, and there he kept her very well." Then a teacher encourages one child to volunteer to sing the saying all the way through without interruption. The other children are asked to listen carefully and imitate the melody the child sings. Continue this game as long as the children volunteer to sing the saying.

If the children already have some technical readiness with the bar instruments, they may also play the rhythm of the text on the instruments, once again playing the whole song through. The other children then sing or play in imitation of the improvisation. In concentrating on the tones used in the melody, the children make a transition to assignment (b).

a)2 To counter-balance metric (beat-restricted) improvisation, practice "singing-narration." A familiar fairy tale can provide the most suitable text. ("Once upon a time there was a king. He was poor, but he had a beautiful daughter." -- "Rumpelstiltskin") The tempo of this narration is *fluid*. Narrate the text by singing it, without stipulating a certain range of tones. Once again, ask for volunteers, then have the rest imitate the improvisation. The children will usually arrive at a recitation-style by themselves, whereby they recite the

text on a main tone and emphasize important words or syllables by a higher or lower tone, closing with a definite downward step. The teacher may lead them carefully to this style by praising children who arrive at this solution, and pointing out that "Singing Narration" does not mean a song or a melody, but indicates speech that is sung, or "spoken singing."

a)2_1 After starting with syllabic recitative (every syllable receives one tone), introduce smaller and larger *melismas*. Some children may have already discovered

melismas in their first attempts at "singing narration." In the sample text above, melismas are appropriate on the words "King" and "daughter."

b)1 Use texts such as those in exercises a)1 and a)2, but limit the range of tones which may be used. At first restrict the range to two tones, then increase it gradually to three, four and five tones. Try out all possible intervals in the pentatonic. For example, in a two-note range g-a, g-c (fourth), e-g, f-c (fifth), or d-a. Transposing is always allowed, and is indeed required whenever a child is limited by his own vocal range. Name a "main tone" the "Finalis" and a counter-tone the "Tenor," especially when using ranges of three to five tones. At first the initial and final tones are the same. Chose the modes so they can be grasped and mastered by the children. (Don't give up immediately if it takes a little effort for them to learn certain idioms and keep them in mind.) (For example, in the "re-mode": d-e-g-a-c)

Name a main tone and counter tone (Finalis and Tenor)

b)2 In singing narration use the counter-tone for reciting and close on the main tone.

Recite on the tenor

b)1$_1$ Textual rhythmic patterns progress in the same way as did the rhythmic exercises. (See I, 5 and II, 5 and 6.) Broaden the tonal range to include 6 and 7 tone rows in the various modes.

Rhythmic texts progress as did rhythmic exercises

b)1$_2$ Increasing the tonal resources does not necessarily complicate the tonal structure, nor does adding the half-step. What does complicate the structure are intervals within various ranges, especially those not lying in the customary triadic patterns and its variants (neighbor tones, etc.) For example, the sequence d'-c''-g'-a'-e'-d' would be more difficult than d-e-f -g -a (Lydian). According to one's point of development and ability, different exercises in unfamiliar ranges and rows may now be tried out, and later used in improvising melodies.

Complicating tonal structure depends on combination of intervals used

b)2$_1$ It is possible to use rhythmic patterns instead of texts as a basis for inventing melodies. When this is done, all of the exercises developed for rhythm can be used again for making melodies. (Folksong texts may be abstracted into their rhythmic components and then given new melodies.)

Rhythmic models without text as a basic for melody

2. Exercises in completing melodies
a) in formal periodic structure (see exercises in completing rhythmic forms under II)
b) in aperiodic ("spun-out") form, and free-dialogue and "bow" forms. (see II, 10)
Procedure:
a)1 Echo-playing as a preparatory exercise: The teacher plays a two-beat motive on a bar instrument using two

**Completing me-
lodies with peri-
odic and aperiodic
structures**

Melodic echo-playing

59

analogous to rhythmic exercises	to five tones. The group echoes the motive. The teacher finishes after 2, 4, or 8 motives by returning to the original tone. The entire piece is played over an ostinato or bordun which regulates the tempo, played by the whole group. The method here is the same as that in the rhythmic exercises found under I, 3a and 3b: first the whole group, then individuals, then "exchange roles."

a)2 Using the principle of echo-playing one can practice completing melodies with various closing formulas. The teacher starts with a two-beat motive. The students echo it. The teacher adds a "spun-out" (i.e. not final) motive, and the students answer it by creating a closing turn, returning to the original tone.

Playing echoes becomes an exercise in completing melodies

a)3 The teacher gives a *four-beat* statement which moves from the original tone upward to the counter-tone. The students answer with a downward-moving motive. (Use either bar instruments or vocal syllables "ma" or "la.") *Stipulation:* The student should refer to the motives of the opening statement, either picking up and using the rhythm of the opening motive, or "spinning out" the arch of the melody.

Opening motive
or
Melodic arch

a)4 Here the methodological structure involved is like that of the rhythmic exercises. (See II: 3 — 9)

In middle sections (eg. B in the reprise form AABA) the initial tone is the counter-tone rather than the main tone. (In authentic modes V instead of I). Instead of an answer, an echo is used to emphasize the transitory quality of such middle sections. (See II, 6 for extending and breaking through periodic structure.) In melodic construction, especially when adding a coda at the end, omit the final tone and do not use it until the very end. For example, use deceptive cadences ending on the second or fourth. When the final tone is reached in the coda, a true feeling of closure and finality is accomplished. Completing and improvising melodies (the second occurs when a monologue has developed out of a dialogue), should take place in *every key* and *every mode*.

B-section starts
of V

Avoid final tone
before coda

every key
every mode

b)1 The teacher plays or sings a melodic arch in a neutral or freely flowing rhythm, giving the impression of a melisma. The students take turns spinning it out, and the

Creating free
melodic arches

last one closes the melody by returning to the opening tone. Regulate the length of a melodic "arch" according to the length of a comfortable breath, (also a good regulator when playing a melodic arch). Carry out this exercise in various keys and pre-determined modes.

b)2 Have the group build an ostinato using an interval of a fifth. Each enters successively with complementary rhythms and motives until the whole group is involved. Then, while they play the ostinato further, they hum and vocalize using the five tones described by the bordun, creating free arches of melody one breath in length. When the whole group has entered there can be an increase in intensity of both dynamics and tone until a climax is signalled and the piece is ended. Or it is possible to "un-build" the texture gradually until only the ostinato remains, continuing to dismantle the piece down to the last (first) player.

Free humming and singing over an ostinato

3. *Melodic variation:*
    a) Coloration (ornamental variations)
    b) Modal transformation of a melody, keeping stable the direction of movement and rhythm
    c) Metric and rhythmic variations of a stable melody
    d) Free variation including complete change of structure
    e) Ostinato variations (Chaconne)

Coloration, modal change, metric-rhythmic variation, free variations

Chaconne

Procedure:
a) Begin with simple ornamentations of folk songs, using recorders, bar instruments, the voice. Gradually make the variations richer, retaining the main tones of the melody and working only in unison. Other students can keep playing the basic melody.
Different colorations may be used simultaneously (heterophony). In addition to adding ornamental embellishments and sub-divisions (passing tones, neighbor tones, modulating tones), it is possible to simplify the melody. This is accomplished by holding out a melodic tone, or using only the outermost or most characteristic tones in the melody, especially when the melody is played on instruments that have a lot of reverberation, or on stringed instruments.

Coloration

Heterophony

Simplify melody by holding out main tones

b) Modal transformation means making the melody conform to a different mode. From a Dorian melody one can derive a Myxolydian melody, not by changing only a few tones, but by adjusting the entire melody. In this exercise only the direction of the notes and the rhythm are retained. Small departures from the original are completely allowed if they result in better expression in the new mode.

Modal transformation: making the melody fit the new mode

c) Sing or play the tones of the melody, but in a completely neutral rhythm. These tones may then be given a different rhythmic structure. A triple meter may be made out of what was originally a duple melody. Pay careful attention to correct prosody. Constantly changing meters are possible. Experiment, too, with mensurated and free rhythmic structure and use other subdivision possibilities.

Neutral rhythmics new meters and rhythms Prosody

d) Free variation is derived from a synthesis of the above exercises (a) through (c).

e) Work out a four or eight-beat ostinato. Above it individuals, and later the whole group, can improvise melodically. When the group improvises together, be sure every individual melody continues to be heard while the following variations are added. Pay attention to the key, and be sure each new variation corresponds tonally and rhythmically with its predecessor. Experiment with rhythmic and vocal improvisation.

V. IMPROVISING MUSICAL PIECES:

1. Establishing melodies:
a) modal structure
b) cadencing structure

Procedure:
a) Construct modal five and seven-tone melodies (structures), denoted by one single characteristic tonal field of reference, and containing no alternating changes of function (harmonic cadences) by using the *pedal point* (extended tone), *bordun* (bass interval of a fifth, and its variations), or *ostinato* (recurring accompaniment motive). Chose "swinging" ("waving") borduns and the ostinato figures developed from them so their outward movement contrasts with the movement of the melody. They should not run parallel to each other in their general contours. The same holds true for the

Pedal point Bordun Ostinato "Swinging" bordun and ostinato motives contrast in movement to the melody

rhythmic-motivic structure of the accompaniment. (The progression of the rhythm and melody is further discussed under the title *Registration*, V, 2).

(The progression of the rhythm and melody is further discussed under the title *Registration*, V, 2).

Cadencing melodies

Fundamental tone
voice-leading as a
real counter voice
Omit parallel oc-
taves and fifths
Other voices are
mere registration

Lesson progression

b) Melodies with clearly cadencing structure (major, harmonic minor) should be accompanied with the simplest use of elementary harmonic functions. The bass (or fundamental) voice-leading becomes in this case a real counter-voice to the melody. As such it must follow the rules for correct voice-leading which preclude parallel movement in octaves and fifths. The other voices are not yet handled as "real" voices, but merely add to the registration of the counter-voice. Thus, they may move in parallel with it.

This lesson can be constructed progressively in the following manner:

1) Basic tones of
function only at
the start of new
function area

Hand signs as
an aid

1) Accompany the melody using only the fundamental tones of the basic functions (tonic, dominant, sub-dominant), playing only where the harmonic function changes in the melody. (Strike the instrument at the beginning of the piece and thereafter only when the function changes.) Let the children find the correct places themselves. If they are not immediately successful, use hand signs to indicate the functions. Have one child who hears correctly give the hand signs to the group.

Adding rhythm

2) Add rhythm to the harmonic progression of fundamental tones. (Strike the instruments several times during the space of one harmonic function.) Follow the examples and patterns already explained in the rhythmic exercises to develop the rhythm (complementary rhythms, sub-divided figures, etc.).

Adding intervals
and chords

3) Expand the progression of fundamental tones to two and three-note chord progressions. (Add 8, 5 and 3 to the tonic, 7 to the dominant, and 6 to the subdominant.)

Figuration

4) Add figuration to the chordal progression by breaking up the chords into individual notes.

Adding melody

5) Add melody to the functional progression, adding new melodies over old over the same harmonic structure in the style of the "Quodlibet."

63

Registration, Articulation	**2. Registration and articulation of:**
	   a) modal melodies
	   b) cadencing melodies

Procedure:

a)1 By "registration" we mean the process of adding voices to the melody which run in precise parallel either above or below it. The goal is sonorous coloration and instrumentation of the melody. The instruments most suited for "registration" are those with voices higher or lower by an octave or a fifth, or, especially effective, by an octave extention of the twelfth. Lower fourths and other intervals resist exact (real) parallel voice-leading, and should be used only when one takes into account the danger of "mannerisms", (eg. parallel major thirds, parallel minor sevenths). Careful listening and experimentation with different instruments will prevent stylistic exaggeration.

Registration by real parallel voices

a)2 By "articulation" we mean relaxing the ground plan of parallel movement (paraphony) through deviations which favor the tonality or modal structure. When thirds and sixth chords move in parallel (fauxbourdon) their quality alternates between major and minor intervals according to the mode in use. When thirds and sixths are inverted their quality changes, whereas fifths and fourths remain "perfect" when inverted, even if the mode in use inclines generally toward augmented or diminished intervals. Thus, fifths and fourths are retained in real parallel voice-leading. Registration can change from formal section to formal section, or at specified places. (It is best if step-wise melodic movement is varied with leaps and repeated tones.) For example, a sequence of triads may change to a series of sixth chords, and vice versa. This should not happen so often, however, that the basic paraphonic structure is challenged. The same is true for heterophonic variations (See "variations" IV, 3). These also constitute a form of "articulation."

Articulation by deviating from real parallel movement in thirds and sixths

Change registration at appropriate places according to formal sections or melodic contour

Paraphony and heterophony must still be heard

a)3 Directly opposite to consequential paraphony is "diaphony." in which a second voice moves in exact "mirror movement" to the melody. Here, too, deviations in intervals are permissible, but the resulting voice must clearly contrast with a genuine counter-voice, as is found in polyphony or counter-point. It is distinguished by its continual opposing movement.

"Mirror-movement" ("Diaphony")

64

Cadencing melodies are rarely registered, but they can be articulated, made more sonorous, with thicker texture by adding extra voices to the melody. These voices have their source in the functions of the melody itself; they move as much as possible in parallel with it, with only a few deviations from absolute parallel voice-leading according to the basic harmony. This is the principle of the polyphony of central European folksong and yodelling. The texture is made to be as thick as possible. The purest result comes from settings for *three voices*. An example, the internationally known Christmas carol: "Still, still, still weil's Kindlein schlafen will" in F-major. The main voice singing the broken triad c-f, a-c, f- f-a-g, g-b-flat-e, c- e-g-f, etc. The second voice follows the first one third lower, as parallel as possible, but following the harmonic progression marked out by the first voice: a-c, f-a, c, c-f-e, e-g-c, c-e-c. The third voice: f-a, c-f, a, a-c-c, c-d-g, g-c-a.

The *fauxbourdon* technique can also provide a possible way to articulate cadencing melodies, ("chordal type melodies"), especially those with mainly step-wise movement. Here a rule for the modal fauxbourdon, that fourths always are "perfect", may be set aside at the cadences, for example in the closing cadence d-f-b, e-g-c, (thinking from the lower note up). In such cases the augmented fourth of the dominant remains.

Articulating cadencing melodies by making their textures thicker and more sonorous

Middle-European polyphony

Fauxbourdon

Dominant chord remains

VI. DRAMATIC PLAY

Don't compose, combine elements in improvisation

Use all forms of improvisation to create dramatic "scenes." The scene itself should not be "composed," but develop naturally through improvisation in language, music, and movement.

The text may come from a fairy tale, the Christmas story, sayings and little spoken pieces. The contents should be appropriate for the age group of the children involved. When no public performance is planned, have the children sit in a circle, facing inward, so the action of the play may take place in their midst. For performances use a half-circle.

Play in a circle

"Epic" parts of the story will be recited, since they relate the progress of the story. Use the technique of "singing narration" for this, done either by an individual or the entire group.

| Introduction | An introduction can be developed from the title itself, if it is given rhythm and chanted ("Rumpelstiltskin, Rumpelstiltskin, Rumpelstiltskin, Rummm!!"). Repeat this section, then "Oh, how fine that no one knows, that here Rumpelstiltskin goes!" (section B), followed by a reprise. The text is whispered, and may later be omitted when a melody has been created on the instruments. |

As symbol-bearers, introduce:

| Tone color | 1. *Tone color:* (Chose a certain appropriate instrument to accompany a certain figure: metallophone and tambourine for the king, bass xylophone for the miller, alto or soprano xylophone for his daughter, rattle and wood block for Rumpelstiltskin, glockenspiel for the tears of the weeping queen.) |

| Rhythmic motives | 2. *Rhythmic motives:* (slow stepping rhythm for the miller, pathetic rhythm for the king, springing or skipping rhythm for Rumpelstiltskin.) |

| Melodic and tonal motives | 3. *Melodic and tonal motives:* (ascending minor seconds or fourths for the poor miller; fifth — octave, or triadic fanfare for the king; speaking sound for Rumpelstiltskin; weeping figure of descending seconds sung or played on a recorder, perhaps reinforced by a second voice in thirds or, even sharper, in parallel seconds, for the miller's daughter; xylophone "teardrops"; later, when Rumpelstiltskin wants to take the child, glockenspiel "teardrops" for the queen.) |

All the motives are introduced at first as ostinati, and later coupled with the correct figure, who also moves in an appropriate way. Use "singing narration" to present the dialogue in the scene, while the text is being recited.

| Transitions and interludes | The opportunity to have purely instrumental interludes comes during transitions or to indicate passing time. (The latter may be symbolized through circular figures and gong tones, while the text is being recited.) |

| Work out questions together with children Masks and costumes only after characterizations worked out through movement and gesture | All of these considerations should be decided with the children. Every child should receive a task, and it is recommended that several children share one task. Introduce masks and costumes only *after* the children have worked out descriptive movements and gestures. Avoid exaggeration or elaborate equipment; a small suggestion of character should suffice. |

Child directs
Performance with-
out teacher

One child should direct the music group, and all of the performances should be able to take place entirely without the presence of the teacher.

Stay within the
elementary

In scenic play it is enough to stay within the borders of elementary music and forms of dance. Do not trespass in the direction of the artistic theater, ballet, and the opera.